# LESSONS IN
# LOYALTY

## How Southwest Airlines Does It –
## An Insider's View

# LORRAINE GRUBBS-WEST

# LESSONS IN
# LOYALTY

## How Southwest Airlines Does It –
## An Insider's View

Printed in the United States of America
ISBN: 0-9762528-5-6

*Credits*
Editor                                         Alice Adams
Design, art direction and production    Melissa Monogue, Back Porch Creative, Plano, TX
                                                      info@BackPorchCreative.com

# Contents

*Southwest Airlines ...*

One of the Top Five Best Companies to
Work for in America (Fortune Magazine)

———————————

Fewest customer complaints 18 years in a row
(DOT Air Travel Consumer Report)

———————————

Profitable 31 consecutive years

———————————

#2 Most Admired Company in America
(Fortune Magazine)

———————————

Employee turnover rate averages less than 10%

———————————

A $10,000 investment in 1972 would
be worth more than $10 million today

# *How do they do that?*

# How do they do that?

*I*n an industry rife with bankruptcies, layoffs, furloughs and high oil prices ... along with being labor intensive and ultra sensitive to the unpredictable waves of the economy, one thing has been consistent for the past 30 years ... Southwest Airlines has been a winner.

What does Southwest do so differently, allowing them to prosper while so many of the long-established airlines have disappeared?

Southwest and its competitors have all been led by top executives who make logical strategic decisions, develop strong brand images, create enticing customer incentives, and hire talented people – all of the elements for success.

But, what separates Southwest from the rest of the pack is the strong employee and customer loyalty it has developed – a feeling of devotion, duty and attachment to Southwest.

*Lessons in Loyalty* is written from one former employee's perspective. It is the inside story of life and work at Southwest Airlines. It's a story packed with creative ideas that you can take and implement in your own organization ... today! You will learn lessons about:

• How organizations, who realize they are in the people business rather than the airline business, manufacturing or insurance business, can develop a deep loyalty leading to long-term, sustained success.

- Implementing a corporate strategy that creates an amazing culture where people who "fit" will clamor to be a part of your company.

- Celebrating team victories and individual accomplishments, creating an environment where everyone works together to accomplish more.

- Becoming the best in customer service and staying on top because you have trusted, loved and laughed with your employees and have empowered them to do the same with your customers.

- Understanding that building good relationships with employees has little to do with whether or not the company is unionized (over 80% of Southwest Airlines' employees are unionized).

- Providing a platform, tools and training where people are dedicated to making a difference because they believe in and trust the management team.

In this book, I have identified nine "loyalty lessons" learned throughout my experience at Southwest, and regardless of your organization or your corporate culture, I believe these lessons are applicable and can make a positive difference. You won't have to wait on your CEO to implement these lessons. You can begin right now – wherever you are – and you will see the results.

I invite you to read my story. …

# *Loyalty* #*1*
## Lesson

## Hire Attitude – Train Skills

"**H**erb Kelleher!" the emcee bellowed, and the hushed crowd roared to its feet.

The popular CEO of Southwest Airlines had just been named to receive the Houston Chamber of Commerce's Aviation Person of the Year award, and the audience's approval was obvious.

When Kelleher took the podium, his words were simultaneously astonishing to those who didn't know him and delightfully anticipated by those who did. "Would everyone please hold your applause?" he asked. When the ballroom had silenced, he continued. "Now, if there is anyone in the audience who works for Southwest Airlines, would you please stand?"

Several stood and the sincerity of the CEO's request was obvious to the audience: "Please direct your applause to **these** people because **they** are the ones who have earned this award. I'm simply here to pick it up."

I was in the crowd that day – 15 years ago – and suddenly, without warning, I was hooked. "How incredible it would be to work for a company like that!" I thought almost out loud.

I had enjoyed operating my own aviation charter business, but after 10 years of blood, sweat and tears for 24/7, I knew I was ready for a change … and the seed had been planted. Herb Kelleher had quite aptly conveyed the very heart and spirit of Southwest Airlines that day and I wanted to work for his company!

Southwest's phenomenal culture has raised the bar for loyalty in American business. The question is, how did it happen? How does one go about creating that type of environment in companies today?

In a heartbeat, Southwest Airlines executives – starting with Herb Kelleher, himself – will tell you their people and their uncommon loyalty to the company perpetuate the culture. The solidarity among employees is astounding. Their commitment to the company is unparalleled, and their productivity and customer service are legendary.

Without a doubt, the culture is rooted in the company's past and has filtered down through its leadership. Somehow, Kelleher and company continue to attract approximately 31,000 of the "right" kind of people – those who delight in each other, their employer and their customers.

I watched Herb Kelleher accomplish that very thing at the Chamber luncheon that day by putting the first principle into practice:

## *Principle #1:*
## **Make them want you before you want them.**

Southwest Airlines is masterful at putting its message out to the applying public:

> "If you want to have fun, this is the place to work! This is a place where you can be yourself, where it's okay to be irreverent, where you will be loved and valued, where Elvis has been spotted (Herb Kelleher in costume, no less), and where 'wearing pants is optional!' (Of course, some sort of outer clothing is required, but it's not at all unusual to see flight attendants wearing khaki shorts and Polo shirts.)"

The company's employment ads mirror the same company philosophy declared in its marketing ads:

> "We at Southwest Airlines foster and embrace fun, creativity, individuality and empowerment. We love our employees. We trust our employees. Our employees, in turn, work very hard, give "Positively Outrageous Service" (POS) to our customers, and make it possible to keep our fares consistently lower than the competition's."

> Now I ask you, who *wouldn't* want to work for Southwest Airlines?

Critics might suggest that Southwest attracts only party people, not career seekers, but the statistics prove those critics dead wrong.

Turnover is very low and efficiency is high. Case in point: Southwest received the highest ratings five years in a row in the three customer-service categories rated by the U.S. Department of Transportation (DOT) – fewest customer complaints, smallest number of mishandled bags and best on-time performance. (Internally, the company quickly dubbed this recognition the "Triple Crown Award" and capitalized on it, PR-wise.)

Some months after the luncheon where I first became acquainted with Herb Kelleher, I was heading a Chamber committee charged with planning a celebration of aviation at Hobby Airport in Houston through an event called HobbyFest. A representative of Southwest Airlines' Marketing Department was serving on the same committee.

Arriving late to a meeting several weeks later, the Southwest employee apologized and explained she was extremely busy due to a number of open positions. She also casually mentioned she was looking to fill a couple of vacancies in her department and then finagled a way for the two of us to work together on this committee … and the rest, as they say, is history.

I, like others sitting in the Chamber luncheon audience that day, had made it my mission to go to work for Southwest Airlines. As a result of the HobbyFest committee, I got that chance and was soon hired in its Marketing Department. Thus began my incredibly fun, creative, crazy, productive and immensely rewarding journey with Southwest Airlines.

Not everyone who wants to work at Southwest Airlines gets to, of course. Unlike many Fortune 500 companies that require advanced degrees, strict dress codes and a strictly defined "professional" demeanor, Southwest advertises that "professionals need not apply."

Southwest chooses its employees carefully because its culture is unique and fiercely protected. Rather than being a megacorporation with thousands of employees, Southwest is a large family with many members. Potential Southwest employees are those who exhibit a fun-loving, hard-working, caring and giving spirit. They are people who want to make a difference in the lives of others and, at the same time, want to feel appreciated and valued themselves.

At Southwest Airlines, people are hired for their attitude and trained for the skills they'll need to do their jobs. Money is seldom a motivator. In fact, many – like me – actually take a cut in pay to work there!

One of the incredible things about working for this company is that you are actually encouraged to explore your interests and talents, find your own niche, and follow great relationships, even if that means moving to other departments.

Periodically, our recruiters would show up on the first day of new-employee training classes and listen as the new people shared where they came from and why they came to work for Southwest Airlines. Listening to the stories of 150 new hires helped us stay true to our mission, making sure we continued hiring the right kind of people to work for the company. Their stories also enabled us to gauge our effectiveness in the second principle:

## *Principle #2:*
## Define the type of employee you want –
## then communicate it.

Employer branding is critical to attracting the right people, and Southwest Airlines has been very successful in defining the kind of people it wants – people who:

- like to think outside the box

- are not afraid to be themselves

- are honest and ethical

- have a high level of integrity

- are good team players

- take their jobs seriously, but can laugh at themselves

Southwest has operated in the southwestern region of the United States for more than three decades and has established an excellent employer-branding image. The public in that area is very familiar with who Southwest is: fun, irreverent, a great place to work, etc., and because of its solid branding, it has had no problem finding the right kind of employees.

However, when Southwest moved into new markets, it discovered a much different scenario. For example, in 2000 when we went to Raleigh-Durham, North Carolina, to meet with various agencies and organizations that had agreed to partner with us to find employees, it was all too obvious that they had no idea who Southwest was. The partners' inability to understand our unique culture was getting in the way of our employee needs. They kept asking, "What skills are you looking for?" to which we continually replied, "We hire for attitude and train for skills." They just weren't getting it.

In one of those epiphany moments, I realized they probably would never get it until they experienced the Southwest culture for themselves, so I invited them to come to Dallas to tour our home office and talk to our employees. At the end of that visit, they all said, "We finally get it: *Hire for attitude and train for skills!*"

As I was getting ready to leave Southwest a few months ago, I couldn't help but compare its philosophy about its employees with other companies I had come to know through the Southwest Airlines Speakers' Bureau and various other opportunities.

As I looked out at my department, I glimpsed at one object that had been my view for the past five years: an inflatable cow – udders and all – hanging from the ceiling, someone's cherished cubicle decoration! At Southwest, anything goes – within reason – when employees decorate their workspaces. I loved it!

This may not work for all corporate environments, but allowing employees to take ownership of their workspace was one small way for our company to say, "We trust you."

Perhaps the most extraordinary example of employer branding came just two days after the horrible events of September 11, 2001.

You know the story – all planes were grounded and the U.S. airline industry was in chaos. None of us knew how it would all play out ... would we have jobs or would there even be a Southwest Airlines in the future?

We had advertised a job fair for flight attendants in Houston on September 13, but we wondered if anyone would show up at such an event after 9/11. Not wanting to cancel in case someone did come, we decided to go ahead – and more than 200 people showed up!

Imagine! That many people had decided, "In spite of the horrible circumstances and all the uncertainty, I still want to work for Southwest Airlines." That's employer branding at its best!

## *Principle #3:*
## Tap into Marketing and PR Department strategies to enhance your recruiting efforts.

As with all corporations, the bottom line is of major concern to Southwest Airlines – and its employees lead the way in running a lean operation. They also are fiercely loyal to that end and are constantly working to increase efficiency and save money.

At the same time, Southwest's culture values relationships. Successes are celebrated, individuals are recognized and appreciated, and the family atmosphere prevails. Thus, while the employees of Southwest are fiercely competitive against outside threats, any internal competition happens with the mindset: "I'm competing against a family member, not 'the enemy.'"

Without exception, people work together across departments, which results in Herculean efforts to reach common objectives. A good example of this was a challenge in the People Department in 2000. We wanted to redesign our recruiting strategy to attract potential employees in a tight labor market – at the lowest possible cost. To accomplish this mission, we came up with the idea of partnering with the Marketing Department. They were already out there, putting the Southwest message in ads to potential passengers. Why not tag those ads with our recruiting message?

Sounds simple, right? This one strategy gave our hiring message great exposure with little financial commitment … and it was successful.

Another success was tapping into Southwest's advertising on televised National Football League games. Instead of an ad targeting passengers, viewers saw ads aimed at recruiting and generated enough calls to shut down the phone system at the home office!

To further our employer branding, we began exploring opportunities with the Public Relations Department to create media stories featuring Southwest Airlines employees – like the father and daughter who flew together as a pilot team.

Bottom line – we quickly learned we could leverage our efforts with the experts, thereby helping us accomplish our goals. Once we began the process and the people in these departments understood our mission, they began to think of other ways they could help us.

## *Principle #4:*
## **Make all employees recruiters.**
Southwest Airlines has a network of 31,000 employees, all of whom want to work next to people just like themselves! Southwest Airlines is one of the few companies where you will find an absolutely incredible phenomenon: thousands of employees with enormous individual differences sharing the same values, work ethic and basic character traits. No wonder Southwest's close-knit family atmosphere has continued, even as the airline has expanded operations.

During the interview process, Southwest applicants are tested all along the way. How did they greet the receptionist? How did they relate to other employees they passed in the halls? Because of the amazing esprit de corps that exists at Southwest, these potential employees are unknowingly being "interviewed" all along the way. What they also may not know is that they are easily identified as applicants, so if a candidate is rude to a receptionist, an agent or a member of the maintenance department, that attitude is reported to the recruiter.

The lesson: A candidate who thinks he can "snow" a recruiter during the interview may have already eliminated himself from the interview process because he's proven to other employees that he isn't a "fit" for the system.

## *Principle #5:*
## Determine what's important to your company and design the interview around it.

"Fit" is important when you want to find the "right" people, and the only way to determine who "fits" is to decide what personalities are successful in a particular environment.

At Southwest Airlines, we defined the necessary dimensions: team player, flexible, creative thinker, does not take himself too seriously, etc. We then developed questions around these dimensions, questions designed to ensure that we had the best chance of getting to the "real" person during the interview. For example, we would ask, "Tell us about a time when you used humor to defuse a difficult customer situation." The response would give us insight into the candidate's personality, coping skills and style.

We also brought in a peer and the appropriate supervisor from the hiring department to conduct portions of the interview, making sure the applicant would fit into that particular department's environment.

Interviews at Southwest Airlines were not always conducted in the conventional fashion. Seeking new challenges, I called the Director of the Training Department in the University for People and told her I was very interested in working in that department. She invited me to join her at an event in Dallas the following week. Afterward, I went to dinner with her team, and we began talking and brainstorming. I had no clue that they were actually interviewing me. We had a great time!

The next day she called and asked me to come in for the *formal* interview. I got the job!

# *Principle #6:*
## Hire "nice" 'cause you can't train "nice."

I cannot overemphasize the principle of hiring "nice" 'cause you can't train "nice." When you're hiring "nice," you're looking for people who:

- can get along with others

- want to be there

- have a desire to do a good job

- have values that match the organization

As a result of hiring nice people, Southwest employees are recognized as being approachable, creating a good first impression, being humble, caring and compassionate, having energy and drive that perform well in a fast-paced environment – all because they are genuinely nice people, not because they've been trained to have these skills. Remember, you can't train "nice."

## *Loyalty* # *1*
## Lesson

### Hire Attitude – Train Skills

## *Loyalty*Principles

*#1* | Make them want you before you want them.

*#2* | Define the type of employee you want – then communicate it.

*#3* | Tap into Marketing and PR Department strategies to enhance your recruiting efforts.

*#4* | Make all employees recruiters.

*#5* | Determine what's important to your company and design the interview around it.

*#6* | Hire "nice," 'cause you can't train "nice."

# *Loyalty* #2
## Lesson

## Immerse Everyone in the Culture Immediately

"We're having a what? A pancake breakfast?"

My smiling coworker replied, "In your honor!"

I should have known. This is *Southwest Airlines*! Though I was not a new Southwest employee, I was new to that department and that was how new employees were treated – special!

I had just stepped off an airplane from Houston, thrilled to be starting my first day on the job in the University for People at Southwest Airlines' home office.

The *entire 25-person staff* at the University for People, I had just been advised, had all contributed to the breakfast (griddle, pancake mix, syrup, fruit, baked goods, etc.) in honor of two other department new hires and me. The plan – we would spend time getting to know each other and then tour the new University for People facilities.

It was an incredible welcome – and clearly demonstrated the first principle involved in sharing the culture right from the start:

# *Principle #1:*
## Establish an environment that helps new employees immediately identify with the company and makes them feel special.

On more than one occasion, I've been asked, "How can an entire department take off work for a pancake breakfast?" At Southwest Airlines, the real question is: "How can they afford *not* to?"

The moment new employees walk in the door, they experience the Southwest Airlines culture, a culture *embraced and fostered from the top down*. They immediately realize they are part of a team – not just another employee. Therein lies a major – and powerful – difference between Southwest Airlines and other companies.

Southwest's employees truly esteem and celebrate people. It's one of those basic values that holds the culture intact. It's an attitude that spills over into everything they do – and the "trickle-down effect" is astonishing.

Right away, new employees realize they are special and their jobs are not "just a job." This instills a sense of pride from the moment they report to work – pride in being chosen to work for a company with a heart, pride in making the right decision to work for Southwest Airlines. As a result, many look at their jobs as more of a *cause* than a place to work … and they relish being part of a large family with many members to care for, customers included.

At the University for People, we made it a point to let our team know when a new team member was hired. We would e-mail or call the new hires at home prior to their start dates to introduce ourselves and welcome them to the team. We got nothing but great feedback on this practice.

The flight attendants took it one step further. Their newly graduated attendants wore a "Help me, I'm new" button for the first few days they flew. It was a great way to get the customers involved in welcoming them (and they were much more patient with the new hire's learning curve!).

The people at Southwest realize the importance of making a positive first impression and spare no effort in making sure new employees feel embraced from the very beginning.

Many employees at Southwest volunteered for a program called "Cohearts," which involved adopting and mentoring a new hire. The "adoptors," or "Cohearts," received a T-shirt bearing the message "Develop an Office Relationship" and proceeded to take the "adoptees" under their wings for six months or longer, making them feel welcome by spending time with them, sending them little gifts, taking them to lunch, etc.

The new employees may or may not have been in the same department, or even in the same town, but they were encouraged and supported during a time that could have otherwise been filled with anxiety. Indeed, many lasting relationships were forged through this program.

## *Principle #2:*
## Make orientation a celebration.

New-employee orientation at Southwest Airlines is an awesome celebration. At the University for People, I taught a new-hire orientation class for several years, entitled "You, Southwest and Success" (later renamed "Freedom, Luv and You"), and it gave me the privilege of introducing the new employees to all that was Southwest Airlines: the wonderful culture, the concepts and values, and the many benefits.

In orientation, the new hires learned they were, indeed, special as they had been chosen over thousands of other applicants. *They were the best, and they were now members of our family – and that was great cause for celebration.*

I'll never forget walking into my own new-hire orientation in 1989. There were balloons floating all over the room, confetti littering the tables, colorful posters decorating the walls, and fun music blaring. The instructor met us at the door and warmly welcomed each of us individually – all 80 of us! It was hard not to be excited.

There were games and videos – like "A Day in the Life of Southwest," depicting the different work groups doing their jobs at warp speed. Another – "The Southwest Shuffle" – featured groups of employees from all over the company describing what their departments did, while dancing and singing to a rap beat, led by none other than

Herb Kelleher, who was introduced as the "Chairman and Chief DJ"!

Dancing and rapping, he sang, "My name is Herb, Big Daddyo. You all know me, I run this show! But without your help, there'd be no love – on the ground or in the air above."

We received a copy of *Our Colorful Leaders* – a coloring book that introduced the company's leaders, pictured in costumes or humorous settings, and told about their personal traits in a unique way.

It did not take us long to recognize that these were not your normal, run-of-the-mill leaders!

Orientation also included more serious messages, such as "The Critical Difference," a video that opened with the camera panning the airplane graveyard in the Mojave Desert. As the camera pans the different aircraft (complete with a mournful howling wind in the background), it zooms in on the broken fuselages of Braniff, Eastern and Pan Am.

Then the host interviews current Southwest employees who previously worked at those now-defunct airlines, asking them to share what it was like to have been working for those airlines when they went out of business. Even after many years, their pain was still evident.

The next segment of the video included interviews with customers who had bad experiences on airlines. The viewer is totally surprised at the end of the video to discover that the disgruntled customers are talking about bad experiences on Southwest Airlines!

So, while the orientation experience was fun and frivolous, there was a definite message of seriousness as well. In the beginning of the video showing the work groups working at warp speed ("A Day in the Life of Southwest"), a message pans that is a direct quote from *The 100 Best Companies to Work for in America* (Robert Levering/ Milton Moskowitz). It says, "It's a blast to work here. You may work your tail off." The video ends with that quote amended by Herb Kelleher: "It's a blast to work here. You *will* work your tail off!"

At the end of our orientation, we took the balloons from the room down into the terminal and gave them to children who were traveling with Southwest. I thought it was great – an immediate chance to interact with our customers in a warm, fuzzy way.

Sharing the company culture is a large part of the indoctrination and, as a result, new employees waste no time putting the culture into action.

The bottom line? As soon as new employees walked in the door, we gave them a reason to believe they had found a home away from home. We wanted to provide a bonding experience as quickly as possible so they would begin embracing the Southwest Airlines culture.

I remember thinking, shortly after being hired, that I had finally found a workplace where I really belonged.

## *Principle #3:*
## Train tough, but with heart.

For obvious reasons, training in the airline business must have very high standards. Training standards *should* be high in any competitive company striving for excellence. However, the Southwest Airlines culture does not stop at the training room door. No matter how tough the training gets, there is still room for compassion and fun – within reason, of course.

As you would guess, the Southwest Airlines training classes are full of fun and games. But make no mistake – the training is as rigorous as you'll find anywhere. All participants are told repeatedly that on-time performance is paramount to passing the class. Periodically, nonbelievers would stay out partying the night before, only to be released from training due to their five-minute tardiness.

Adhering to our superior standards caused our failure rate to be high at times, but we could not allow the undisciplined behavior to invade our environment.

Conducting many exit interviews during my tenure in the People Department, I found some people who thought we were too strict. Yes, Southwest is a company with a big heart, but it also has a mind for discipline and hard work as well. We put every possible support in place to help trainees succeed, and we worked with those who were truly sincere and put forth the effort.

When one individual was hired into a frontline position he simply was not able to do, his managers struggled to help him because he was making such a sincere effort and had such a great attitude. Ultimately, they found another opportunity within their department that better fit his qualifications and skills.

Southwest has impeccable standards in the workplace, and those standards are taught and strictly upheld in all areas, beginning with training. Those who cannot commit to the rigorous standards either self-eject or are asked to leave. Those who meet or exceed the standards go on to reap the rewards of fulfilling and enriching careers.

## *Principle #4:*
## It's smart to test the water to determine if new employees are really the right fit.

Is every employee successful at Southwest Airlines?

Most are, but even with its highly effective screening techniques and discerning training processes, a "wrong fit" slips through the cracks from time to time. For that reason, all new employees are put on a minimum of six months' probation. Anyone can fake it for a week or two, but it's hard to fake it for six months.

I know from firsthand experience, however, that Southwest's heart beats loudly even during the probation period. My third day in the Marketing Department, I was given a copy of the department's marketing manual, the contents of which were highly confidential and heavily guarded – and promptly misplaced it.

On my first day at work, my boss had given me her home telephone number and insisted that I call her anytime if I needed anything. So, after retracing my steps and a thorough search, I called her *at 11:00 that night* and sought her advice.

Losing the notebook was not a good thing, she agreed, but also assured me I was not going to lose my job and she would help me look for the book on Monday. With that call, she gained an even more determined and dedicated employee. (To this day, the book has not been located.)

The leaders and managers at Southwest Airlines realize new employees – and even those not so new – are going to make mistakes, but they watch effort and sincerity closely during the probation period. If a person's intent is to help the customer but something goes awry, the error is forgiven – as long as the person was willing to learn from the mistake.

Like most companies, during the probation period, some new employees fall by the wayside, but most of the employees hired by Southwest Airlines are just the right fit and pass probation with flying colors.

In fact, passing probation was a HUGE thing at Southwest. At the end of an employee's probationary period, he or she would receive a pin, often with a ceremony commemorating this auspicious event. When flight attendants passed probation, their supervisors would meet them at the door of the aircraft, make the announcement and attach their pins in front of all the passengers.

Making employees feel special the moment they walk in the door but forgiving and tolerating honest mistakes helps Southwest employees learn to trust the company. For most of us, there was not a magic "aha" moment when we finally "got" the culture. It was all the little things we saw on a daily basis that drew us in and made us dedicated Southwest employees.

# *Loyalty #*2
# Lesson

## Immerse Everyone in the Culture Immediately

# *Loyalty*Principles

*#1* Establish an environment that helps new employees immediately identify with the company and makes them feel special.

*#2* Make orientation a celebration.

*#3* Train tough, but with heart.

*#4* It's smart to test the water to determine if new employees are really the right fit.

# *Loyalty* **#3**
# **Lesson**

# Keep 'Em Learning

Authors Jon Katzenbach and Douglas Smith wrote the book *The Wisdom of Teams: Creating the High-Performance Organization*, in which they featured several companies, including Southwest Airlines.

One day, the director of the University for People received a call from Katzenbach: "You are going to think I'm absolutely crazy, but I think Southwest Airlines has a lot in common with another organization, and I would like to coordinate a leadership summit for the two groups."

Her curiosity piqued, the director asked, "What organization is it?"

"The U.S. Marine Corps," Katzenbach replied.

What could Southwest Airlines and the U.S. Marine Corps possibly have in common?

As a member of the leadership team selected from Southwest Airlines, we flew to Quantico, Virginia, for a two-day summit ... and, as predicted, we did have several similarities:

- a dedicated workforce

- a disciplined environment

- a strong sense of commemoration and tradition

- a successful track record of achievement in the face of overwhelming odds

The Quantico summit also produced an unexpected benefit from a hiring perspective. Every two years, the Marine Corps advances dedicated, disciplined Marines with ideologies similar to Southwest Airlines employees. Knowing the exiting Marines would make ideal employees, we created a program in which we interviewed any who were interested in coming to work for Southwest Airlines.

We had been doing the same with our pilot hiring for years ... but now we were expanding the program into other work groups.

The Marine summit, an invaluable learning experience, happened as a result of Southwest's belief that we would provide lifelong learning to all employees.

## *Principle #1:*
## Consistently present unique training and learning opportunities to your people.

This principle propelled me to move from the Marketing Department to the University for People and because of Southwest's commitment to this principle, as the company grew, so did the need for more training.

When I joined the University for People, they had outgrown their old training facility and were well underway with expansion plans – plans "outside the box" and way beyond the ordinary.

The space for the new University was an old 40,000-square-foot terminal building with long abandoned jetways. In their usual visionary style, when the University team toured the facility, they didn't see the dirt, dead birds and debris cluttering this neglected area. Instead, they could envision a state-of-the-art training facility consisting of four corridors, each representing an area of the country Southwest serves. The Western section had a cemetery mural depicting the graves of all the airlines that had "bit the dust." One headstone was marked "To be Determined" and represented the next casualty – a poignant reminder to trainees and employees alike that we must not take our success for granted.

This unique facility represented Southwest's fervent commitment to lifelong employee learning. It also clearly conveyed its support of "outside-the-box thinking."

As evidenced by the trip to Quantico, my years at the University for People brought even more unique training and learning opportunities.

During one of those training opportunities, we learned the concept of "Realness," which teaches that in order to learn or understand, one should get as close to the real experience as possible. I immediately thought about the Crisis Committee at Southwest Airlines. We had struggled for years with a unique problem – how do you prepare your employees to handle the worst kind of disaster for an airline – losing an aircraft full of people?

Southwest Airlines boasted an impeccable safety record, and it was hard for our people to relate to the emotions associated with such a tremendous loss of life. The Crisis Committee members understood the concepts in theory but we were missing that real emotional impact necessary to understand the pain and loss we could face at any time.

I applied the "make it real" concept when I invited people who had experienced and survived the loss of a loved one in an airplane accident to come in and talk with our Crisis Committee members. Hearing their brave and emotional stories helped our employees "get it." It was a major breakthrough in the problem we had long been trying to resolve.

Any company can take advantage of the same type of training opportunities we found over the years, so we looked for unique opportunities to strengthen teamwork, support empowerment and give our employees more tools to enhance on-the-job skills.

We also found inexpensive ways to have fun, bond as a team and help the community in the process. During a meeting in San Francisco, for example, we contacted the mayor of the city, told him we had 150 able-bodied volunteers and asked for a project for one day. He arranged for us to go into the inner city and paint the entire YMCA building.

At the end of the day, the graffiti was gone and the building was beautiful. We had worked together as a team and, at the same time, provided a service to the community!

One of the most unique training programs at Southwest was called "Mind the Gap." The leaders of the company had noticed the different work groups at Southwest had begun drifting apart and attitudes like, "That's not my job!" were beginning to appear.

The "Mind the Gap" name was an idea from one of our employees who had just returned from London, where subway riders were constantly reminded to "mind the gap" between the subway and the platform. Since we were looking at "gaps" between work groups, we thought that was an appropriate name for this program.

The "Mind the Gap" program brought together representatives from every work group, and they were asked to tell how they felt their jobs were perceived by the rest of the company.

The female flight attendants, for example, said they felt other people in the company thought they were airheads just looking for husbands or were glorified cocktail waitresses.

Then we asked them to tell us about the reality of their jobs. By the time they were finished, the whole group was in awe. The attendants reminded us how much training they had undergone to learn lifesaving medical procedures and flight regulations; how many hours a day they were on their feet, literally walking miles up and down the aisles of the planes. They talked about how hard it was to be gone from home, how much skill was needed to pacify angry, frustrated, or frightened passengers, and how some of them had saved lives.

This went on through every work group, and at the end of the day, we asked them what we could do to make their jobs better.

One idea from the ramp agent group was to install a chute near the top of the jetway so bags could slide down, rather than being carried down the stairs. This would alleviate the danger of walking up and down stairs in inclement weather.

We reported these great ideas in our company newsletter, *Luv Lines*, so all employees could see that their suggestions were taken seriously.

## *Principle #2:*
## Capitalize on the expertise and experiences of your leaders in employee training.

A leader in our Systems Department had just read Noel Tichy's *The Leadership Engine*, which advocated the concept of leaders sharing their stories with employees, teaching the history of the company and the lessons they have learned. He called to share his discovery.

Taking it from there, we designed a learning program that officially embraced *The Leadership Engine* concepts, although that mindset already existed – unofficially – in the organization.

At Southwest Airlines, you could always find leaders teaching any manner of classes, sharing their expertise and answering employee questions, in spite of their busy schedules. In fact, throughout my time in the University for People, no matter what the training, our leaders supported it and were involved in it.

In the '90s, Southwest Airlines grew very quickly, and we realized many of our employees had been recently hired and didn't have the perspective of the "early days" that the more seasoned employees had.

We wanted these newer employees to hear the stories about Southwest's beginnings from those who had lived them, and because many of the original employees were retiring, we needed to capture and retain the history of the company from their perspectives.

Thus, the "Rocking Chair Sessions" were born. These sessions were held throughout the company during individual department meetings and several original employees or soon-to-be retirees were invited to sit in rocking chairs in front of the group and share stories. Always a big hit, these sessions became routine agenda items.

When we were asked to develop some supervisory training for our newly promoted frontline supervisors, our first objective was to provide them with the real-world tools they would need to be successful. Using "outside-the-box thinking," we developed a program called "Quest," in which every new ground operations supervisor in the company was given three weeks of training, one week at a time at one-month intervals. This type of time commitment to supervisor training was unprecedented!

The first week involved a self-evaluation of the supervisors' leadership strengths and weaknesses. After week one, the supervisors went back to work for a month and were instructed to put together a personal development plan with their managers. When they came back for their second week, they learned skills to motivate and lead teams, including how to write commendation letters.

In week three, they were given more information about the resources available to them via the various departments of the company. During this week we asked them to bring something meaningful to share with the class. Often they would bring pictures of their families, and the sharing of these items created an incredible bond and long-lasting friendships – so much so that many of the classes come back together for a reunion each year!

When existing supervisors heard about the program, they asked to be included – and the "ReQuest" program was developed.

One of my coworkers, struggling with her job for a few months when she went through a ReQuest course, later told me the class had changed her entire attitude about her work. Shortly after graduating from the class and using the tools she had learned, she was promoted to a new position.

## *Principle #3:*
## Make training fun!

One of the top priorities of any training session is to make it fun and interactive. To ensure all participants, including those who were used to very physical jobs, remained engaged and "connected" in a classroom, we spent as much time planning these interactive and fun activities as we spent planning the curriculum.

Our goal was to involve the participants from the moment the class started. The "environmental" team was responsible for the overall fun atmosphere in the classroom. They were instructed to create a theme for the day and develop icebreakers to be delivered anytime they felt the class attention was waning.

The "review" team was responsible for taking the day's material and creating a fun, impactful game, skit or activity to help the participants review and remember the material covered that day.

One review team put together a funeral, complete with casket, candles and solemn music. The facilitators also created games to recognize and celebrate special events in the participants' lives.

Every day, all day long at the University, there was always something fun happening. Sometimes one class would burst in on another class, sing a chant or cheer and then file back out and continue their own class.

One day I was walking down the hall at the University and heard a strange commotion, only to discover one of the instructors had been taped to a table in the classroom and all of his students had gone to lunch!

Sitting in a meeting one day, we suddenly heard music coming down the hall. The door slammed open and the entire group of new-hire pilots walked in with a giant boom box, wearing Hawaiian shirts and singing Jimmy Buffet tunes. They circled the room and then off they went – a regular occurrence at Southwest Airlines!

## *Principle #4:*
## If you find a great book that can be used as a teaching tool, buy enough copies for your entire company.

The executives at Southwest Airlines fervently believe giving copies of great books to their management team – and sometimes to the entire company – is well worth the investment! Why? Because these books offer new ideas, approaches to problem solving, ways of thinking and concepts that can be applied throughout the organization. On several occasions, every employee has received copies of books about motivation, handling adversity, lifelong learning – yet further proof of Southwest's commitment to lifelong learning for its employees.

Talk about walking the walk! Southwest's leaders shout their message loud and clear: Training and learning are crucial at every level, from the top down.

# *Loyalty* **#3**
# **Lesson**

## **Keep 'Em Learning**

# *Loyalty***Principles**

#1 | Consistently present unique training and learning opportunities to your people.

#2 | Capitalize on the expertise and experiences of your leaders in employee training.

#3 | Make training fun!

#4 | If you find a great book that can be used as a teaching tool, buy enough copies for your entire company.

*Loyalty* #**4**
**Lesson**

# People Give as Good as They Get

$A$rriving in Las Vegas for our annual conference, the 150-member Marketing Department was prepared to work for the next three days, setting goals and doing things *normal* companies do at their annual conferences.

It had been a trying quarter.

Southwest Airlines had been removed – overnight – from the nationwide computer reservation systems (CRSs) owned by the other airlines. Because of the exorbitant cost of participating in these CRSs, Southwest had been participating on a limited basis in only one of them. The other airlines had included us in their systems in order to stay competitive. Then, just before Christmas, the competitors had decided – without warning – that they no longer wanted to carry us "free of charge," and we were booted out of their systems.

Our corporate customers instantly lost the ability to book reservations online with Southwest. However, true to Southwest Airlines form, rather than buckling under, we went to work.

Realizing 80 percent of our corporate business came from 20 percent of our customers, the leaders asked the Marketing Department to identify Southwest Airlines' top customers in each city it served and create a system allowing those companies to connect directly into Southwest's computer reservation system – all within a three-week period! We worked 18-hour days to get it done, but we did it.

Now in Las Vegas, we wearily glanced through the agenda items before us: review the legislative agenda, define goals for the year, etc.

Our leaders welcomed us to the conference and then began giving us some very strange instructions. "Take your agenda in your hands like this," they said, "and then tear it down the middle like this. Then tear it again. Then tear it again and throw the pieces in the air."

Ecstatic but confused, we did as instructed.

"Now, that's the extent of the agenda we'll need for the next three days," they continued, "because we are going to do nothing but have fun and celebrate all the hard work you have been doing. We just want you to know how much we appreciate your incredible effort."

Once again, Southwest Airlines proved it was very good at being Southwest Airlines, precisely demonstrating the first principle involved in the "People Give as Good as They Get" lesson:

## *Principle #1:*
## Go to extreme measures to show your employees they are highly valued.

At the very heart of the Southwest Airlines culture is the relationship Southwest has with its employees … and one of its most fundamental tenets is: Employees come first and customers come second.

In fact in 1990, Southwest committed resources to create an internal Culture Committee, a group of 15 employees with the express objective of letting fellow employees know they are appreciated for what they do for the company, day in and day out.

As the company grew, so did the size of the Culture Committee. Today, it has over 120 members!

All work on the Culture Committee is done on the employee's personal time. *The sole purpose of the committee is to do "whatever it takes" to create, enhance and enrich the special spirit and unique culture that has made Southwest Airlines such a wonderful company/family!*

Now, local Culture Committees continue to appreciate employees and also make sure the word gets out any time an employee has a major family event such as a wedding, birth, death, etc., so fellow employees can send cards, flowers, baskets or gifts.

Southwest Airlines also has seven *full-time employees* in the home office, called the "Customer Care Team" (so named because it considers its employees its internal customers) to see that cards, flowers, or gifts are sent for these special employee life events on behalf of the company! Leaders and managers across the system e-mail this group each time they hear of an event in an employee's life.

How far does this caring extend? During a meeting, the vice president of our department asked if any of us had children graduating from college that spring. Three of us raised our hands and our VP wrote down our names and the names of our graduates. Within weeks, each of the grads received a beautiful duffle bag from the company … and if it isn't enough to keep up with the special events in each employee's life, all employees across the system receive four cards a year from the company – mailed to their homes on the date of their company anniversary, their birthday, Valentine's Day and Christmas.

We also solicited our external customers' help in recognizing our employees. One year, we sent "Luv Bucks" – small versions of dollar bills with Herb Kelleher's picture on the front – to each customer in the monthly frequent flyer communication.

In the newsletter, we asked each customer to hand a Luv Buck to any employee they "caught" doing a good job … and our customers got into it in a big way.

Our employees could turn in five "Luv Bucks" for a Southwest Airlines ticket, the program was a big success – and our employees and our customers loved it.

Are you getting the picture? Southwest Airlines is *fanatical* about showing its employees how highly they are valued! It's all about the culture.

Even the new hires are embraced in this extraordinary phenomenon.

Every quarter, a "new-hire roundtable" is held at the home office, and new hires from across the system are chosen to provide feedback in a two-hour, roundtable discussion with the Southwest Airlines CEO and several vice presidents. "Are we the company you thought we were?" they ask, "And how are things going for you?" If they discover they are "missing the boat," they follow up to ensure the situation is rectified.

I had always heard other airlines' cultures were quite different from Southwest's and the day came when I witnessed that difference firsthand. Through a tragic turn of events, a friend who flew for another airline was the copilot on an aircraft that went down, killing everyone on board.

Without hesitation, I rushed to be with his wife. Since she had no family nearby, I became a source of support for her, especially during the first few weeks, and it was then I noticed a big difference in the way the other airline operated. No "official" representative from the airline joined her for almost 24 hours after she had received the news of the crash and her husband's demise.

Accompanying my friend to view the crash site the next day, I could see empathy on the faces of the airline's employees as we walked through the airport, yet none of them came up and spoke to the widow.

Finally, one brave soul walked up and asked if she could hug her. "If this had happened to a Southwest employee," I thought, "the house would have immediately been full of coworkers who would have been taking care of everything! Asking permission to hug someone? What a different culture."

The most valued and meaningful recognition is Southwest's dedication to its employees, which is shown day in and day out in many different ways. The company also has its formal recognition program that includes certain awards for outstanding effort within certain criteria. Employees are nominated by their peers for these special awards and a senior management committee makes the final choices. Some of these include:

1. **The President's Award** – Presented once a year at the annual banquet. The recipients are usually employees who have quietly gone about contributing to the company despite personal challenges, or employees who have consistently gone above and beyond for the company all year long.

2. **The Good Neighbor Award** – Awarded only for significant merit and is not given every year. It is often awarded to a customer or community partner. For example, the year I attended my 10-year banquet, the recipient was an airport director who had been a huge support to Southwest during its start-up service in his city.

3. **The Winning Spirit Award** – A very coveted award, this is given every other month to any number of employees, with the recipients chosen by the CEO of the company. One employee volunteered to keep and care for a customer's dog for several days over the holiday season. The customer had brought the dog to the airport, not realizing that Southwest does not take animals aboard its planes.

4. **Heroes of the Heart** – Given to a behind-the-scenes work group who has gone above and beyond, presented as close to Valentine's Day as possible. The entire group is brought to Dallas to meet with the leaders, given free tickets on Southwest's system, and the name of the employee work group is painted inside a big heart on a Southwest Airlines aircraft.

Each department within the company also creates its own recognition and reward programs.

# *Principle #2:*
## Employee recognition and appreciation produce a very high yield (i.e., Employees give as good as they get).

It all boils down to the age-old law of sowing and reaping. For example, what had created that can-do spirit in the 150 Marketing Department employees in my opening story?

The last sentence of Southwest Airlines' mission statement explains why: "Above all, employees will be provided the same concern, respect and caring attitude within the organization they are expected to share externally with every Southwest customer."

In other words, the leaders at Southwest understand that its employees will "give as good as they get" – and the yield is very high. Employees treat customers with care and compassion because they receive the same from their leaders. It's a Southwest Airlines lifestyle that keeps customers coming back, year after year.

Leaders and managers are taught in training classes to write commendation letters for their employees. Other employees are encouraged to commend their fellow employees, as well. In fact, Southwest tries to make it easy by providing simple forms – called "stroke sheets" – for employees to carry with them so they can quickly fill out a form and extol a fellow employee if they witness something extraordinary an employee has done.

Every time a "stroke sheet" is written, two things happen: First, the person who wrote the letter receives a letter from the company, thanking him or her for commending the employee. Second, the employee being recognized receives a copy of the commendation letter, plus a thank-you from the department head for whatever action he or she performed that generated the original letter.

At Southwest Airlines, we identified "internal" customers as well as "external" customers. The pilots' major internal customers, for example, were the mechanics. Obviously, the planes could not fly unless they were serviced by the mechanics. For the flight attendants, it was the Provisioning Department – they could not do their jobs well if the provisions were not there. Thus, to show their appreciation of their internal customers, departments would "adopt" each other. Every quarter they would do something to show their appreciation. The pilots, regularly showed up at 2:00 a.m. and flipped burgers or cooked barbeque dinners for the mechanics, who worked from 11:00 p.m. to 7:00 a.m.

Actually, by the way Southwest Airlines employees act, you would think they own the company! Well, in essence, they do – about 10 percent of it! The company's profit-sharing plan is one of the most incredible benefits of working for the company.

There is no guarantee the profit-sharing plan will be funded every year – that happens only if the company makes money. But because the employees take ownership in their jobs and take special care to make sure the company *is* profitable each year, the profit-sharing plan has paid very nice sums every year.

As part owners of the company, Southwest's employees are *empowered* to act like owners! Just as employees are encouraged to commend internal customers for doing something for the good of the company, they are also urged to reward external customers for the same thing.

I was standing in line at the gate one day, getting ready to board my daily flight from Dallas to Houston when I overheard two men behind me speaking Spanish. Since I speak the language fluently, I could understand every word they were saying. "I know this is your first time to fly Southwest," said one, "but you are going to love this company. I have flown with Southwest for years. They are a little unique, but there is not a better airline anywhere."

I turned around and spoke to the man in Spanish: "You know, *you* are the reason we are successful at Southwest Airlines and as an employee, I want to thank you and give you a $25-off coupon for your next flight on Southwest."

Of course the man was overjoyed and said to his friend, "See, I told you they were a great company!"

What made me do this? Because *the company empowered all 31,000+ of its employees to recognize and reward even external customers for bolstering the success of Southwest Airlines!*

An interesting sequel to my story about the Spanish-speaking customer: About a year later, I was interviewing a young lady for a position in the University for People, and I asked one of the questions I always ask in an interview, "Why do you want to come to work for Southwest Airlines?"

"Because," she said, "the employees of this company love their jobs. One day last year, my father was traveling …." Incredibly, she relayed the incident with the $25 coupon and her Spanish-speaking father! She said, "He took that coupon, had it framed and put it in his office – and Southwest Airlines will never know how much press they got out of that $25!"

## *Principle #3:*
## Employee recognition and appreciation can be achieved at a surprisingly low cost!

At Southwest Airlines, by using "outside-the-box thinking," we always found ways to celebrate outstanding effort and special events – even for 31,000 employees – without spending millions of dollars!

Remember the annual conference in Las Vegas that ended up being a three-day celebration? Most of that event was sponsored by Southwest Airlines vendors! *It was done at little expense to Southwest!*

The Culture Committee actually created a book of low-to-no-cost ideas submitted by employees. Called *Inventive Incentives,* this book was sent to every leader in the company. The clever ideas in the book included low-cost suggestions such as:

• decorating cubicles for special events

- inexpensive birthday celebrations

- potluck meals

- impromptu volleyball

- softball or basketball games

- perfect attendance lunches

- "Luv Pats" (cards the size of business cards that contained warm messages like "Awesome job!" or "You're terrific!"

The bottom line? It just doesn't cost much to let your employees know how valuable they are. The more they know that, the more valuable they become!

# *Loyalty* #*4*
# Lesson

## People Give as
## Good as They Get

## *Loyalty*Principles

#1 | Go to extreme measures to show your employees that they are highly valued.

#2 | Employee recognition and appreciation produce a very high yield (i.e., employees give as good as they get).

#3 | Employee recognition and appreciation can be achieved at a surprisingly low cost!

*Loyalty* **#5**
**Lesson**

# Find the Kid
# in Everyone

*I* was having the time of my life. The aircraft was coming closer and closer, and I was guiding it in. I had wanted to do this for years!

At the end of my day in the field with the ramp agents, the ramper with whom I had been working was allowing me to have my wish and there I was, standing on a tug so the pilots could see me better, making the gestures with the batons exactly the way the agent was instructing me to do.

He had specifically instructed me beforehand on one particular gesture, and he now said, "Okay, give the signal I taught you." So I started waving the batons in a circular motion, exactly the way he had instructed.

Suddenly, the taxiing aircraft began making a 360-degree turn on the tarmac. I was mortified! What had I done? Of course, about that time, the ramp agent doubled over in laughter. I realized I had been "had." The joke was on me.

When he had asked me at the end of the day if there was anything else I would like to do in his department, I said, "You know, I've always wanted to guide in an aircraft."

He said "No problem. You can guide in our next arrival, due in about 20 minutes." He then proceeded to secretly contact the pilot and tell him there was a "greenhorn" on the ground who would be guiding in the plane. Together, they had concocted the plan, and the pilot had even let the passengers in on the joke. Needless to say, the passengers loved it – and they waved and smiled as they walked off the plane.

Since Southwest Airlines hires people who like to have fun, practical jokes run rampant there. Fortunately, the people who go to work for Southwest are also able to laugh at themselves.

*It's not just that the leaders at Southwest Airlines like to have fun – they realize finding the kid in everyone keeps life from getting too complicated.*

This same philosophy also enables people to take their jobs – but not themselves – too seriously, especially since Southwest demands a lot of its employees, day in and day out. Plus, it relieves stress and empowers employees to diffuse tension with a humor that comes naturally from the "kid" within.

In Proverbs 17:22, the Bible says, "A merry heart does good, like medicine, but a broken spirit dries the bones." Essentially, that describes Southwest's mantra.

A jovial spirit revives and uplifts, looks for the good in everyone and aims to please. A dispirited person is easily offended, keeps score and focuses internally. It's not hard to figure out which type would do whatever it takes to get the job done and make customers happy.

Since Southwest Airlines is full of "merry-hearted" people, it is easy to see why the company is so successful. Here are some of the principles that helped create that success:

## *Principle #1:*
### Let your company's advertising reflect the fun in your company culture.

Most of the advertising messages designed at Southwest Airlines – from the passenger ads to the employment ads – appeal to the "kid" in people. That's because the leaders at Southwest believe it is important for its potential customers and employees to see that part of our culture. The company even created the concept of "fun" fares – fares that were low enough to allow people to go somewhere to have fun – and catchy ads were designed around that concept.

One of Southwest's most famous (or infamous) employment ads showed a flight attendant from the waist down, in a pair of shorts; and the caption read, "Work at a place where wearing pants is optional." It was very successful in attracting the *right* kind of people – fun-loving applicants who would "fit" at Southwest!

When Southwest Airlines opens in a new city, its marketing employees are charged with creating enough craziness and fanfare to ensure that the entire city is aware of its arrival! The Marketing Department's "Light Brigade" marches through the terminals at the city openings, performing hilarious routines with the light batons used to guide in aircraft and all-employee "homemade bands" entertain the public with song.

The addition of service from New Orleans to destinations in newly opened Florida markets was heralded by the appearance of employees in the terminal wearing circa 1920-type bathing suits. Beach ball-tossing contests were used to proclaim Southwest's opening in a California city.

Even the "on-hold" messages on Southwest's telephone system are humorous, ensuring anyone inconvenienced by the hold is entertained. For example, a customer might be listening to a message when an announcer interrupts and says, "Please switch the phone to the other ear, so you can make sure you hear the entire message!"

While fun is a deliberate strategy used as part of the advertising direction at Southwest Airlines, humor is sometimes inappropriate – such as in times of tragedy or national disaster. After 9/11, the fun messages were pulled from the telephone system and the humorous marketing and employment ads were replaced by ads that were more reflective of the national mood. It was several months before the humorous material was reinstated, and then only after the waters had been tested.

## *Principle #2:*
## Incorporate fun in employee training.
## (See Loyalty Lesson #2)

Southwest's training classes are crammed with jokes, lively games and contests (remember the instructor who was taped to the table?) because "fun training" is just as significant to Southwest Airlines as skills training. Since fun and humor are inherent in the character of those hired at Southwest, training classes teach employees to embrace those traits in their relationships with other employees and in dealing with customers.

## *Principle #3:*
## Empower your employees to have fun in communicating with your customers!

Southwest Airlines employees are not expected to "check their personalities at the door." They are given freedom to have fun with the customers and this often takes the form of communicating important information in a humorous way. In-flight announcements and safety information are frequently presented in song.

As a daily commuter, I heard talented flight attendants sing really cute songs and one of my favorites was a rendition of the Oscar Mayer wiener advertising jingle, changed to: "My airline has a first name – it's SOUTH; my airline has a second name – it's WEST. Oh I love to fly it every day, and if you ask me why I'll say, 'cause Southwest Airlines has a way of bringing sunshine to your day!"

One of the flights I was on experienced a somewhat rough landing. The flight attendant came on the PA and apologized for the hard landing. "I checked with the captain and he said it wasn't his fault," she reported. "I checked with the copilot, and he said it wasn't his fault so we are going to determine that it was the 'asphalt.'"

In keeping with its culture and integrity, Southwest not only empowers its employees to have fun with its customers, but it also defends the right of its employees to do so. At one time, Southwest was "brought to task" by the Federal Aviation Administration for presenting the safety announcements in a humorous way. Herb Kelleher came to the flight attendants' defense and asserted that customers actually tend to listen *more* when the information is presented with humor. The challenge was dropped.

Airline customers, by the very nature of the business, often have reason to be disgruntled: weather delays, security requirements, disruptive children and impediments created by their own hectic schedules, or perhaps challenging circumstances that precipitated their travel. Any time masses of customers become disgruntled because of long weather delays, gate environments can become quite volatile, but at Southwest, gate agents are trained to bring out their "humor tricks" at times like this and are generally successful in "finding the kid" in their passengers.

Running silly contests like "Who has the biggest hole in your socks?" agents often have people actually taking off their shoes to look. Or they might play, "Who has the most keys on their key chain," "Who has the most lipsticks in their purse," or "Who has the ugliest driver's license photo."

People love to be entertained, and if their "innermost kids" can be found in stressful times, stressful challenges can become fun adventures!

## *Principle #4:*
## Hire people who can laugh at themselves

Not everyone appreciates a practical joke. Had I not had the ability to laugh at myself and see the humor in the incident I described at the beginning of this chapter, I would have been humiliated. But, being "just like all those other Southwest Airline employees," I enjoyed the laugh just as much as the ramp agents, the pilots and crew, and the passengers!

People who have a great sense of humor will almost always be practical jokers. So, if you have a company full of them – like Southwest Airlines – you never know when one will strike.

As a fairly new employee for Southwest, I was at Houston's Hobby Airport one day when I overheard a pilot tell an operations agent over the two-way radio to call a mechanic because he had experienced a "bird strike." (When a plane strikes a bird, it can result in some pretty serious damage to the plane.) The operations agent called the mechanic, who went rushing over to the aircraft, expecting to find a grave situation. What he found, instead, was a rubber chicken the pilot had plastered to the windshield of the airplane!

Throughout my tenure with Southwest, I provided a number of opportunities for my coworkers to have the last laugh.

Unfortunately, I have a terrible time remembering names – not a good deficit in the Marketing Department where part of your job involves interacting with all the other internal groups.

I frequented the air cargo building, where Ernie worked and I could never remember Ernie's name. About the fourth time I saw him and came up blank when it came time to call his name, he said, "You know, this is getting a little insulting. I have told you my name so many times, and you still can't remember it!"

"Ernie," I promised, "the next time we meet, I am going to know your name!" I immediately went out and bought a book to help me improve my memory.

Equipped with my new knowledge, I walked into the air cargo building and proudly blurted, "Hey, Bert, how is it going?"

Ernie looked at me in disbelief. "Who's Bert?" he asked. "My name is Ernie!" Obviously, I had missed the part of the book admonishing not to try to associate someone's name with a dual name!

For the first 10 years of my career with Southwest, I had heard many stories about people getting on the wrong plane. "Now, who could be stupid enough to do that?" I thought. Then, during the time I commuted to Dallas, I was running late for my plane back to Houston one evening. I was flying on a "non-rev, employee-fourth" ticket (a non-paying ticket that allowed me to take the fourth flight attendant's seat).

Sometimes, if the plane was not full, an employee with this type of ticket could sit in a regular seat unless it was needed for a passenger.

But the operations agent had told me the flight on which I was scheduled was pretty full, and that I should go ahead and take the flight attendant's seat.

Needing to make a quick phone call before I boarded, my cell phone battery was suddenly low, so I headed for the nearest public telephone. I was on the phone when I heard my flight announced.

I rushed to the plane and boarded, being careful to sit in the fourth flight attendant's seat. The flight attendant sitting by me said, "It looks like the plane is not going to fill up. Why don't you take a seat in the back and if we need it, we'll let you know."

"That's funny," I thought, "they told me this flight would be full."

I ended up sitting next to a gentleman and when the flight attendant making the announcements said, "Ladies and gentlemen, welcome aboard our 50-minute flight to San Antonio," I turned to him and said, "You know these flight attendants are so funny, aren't they? They just love these practical jokes!"

"What are you talking about?" he asked.

"We're not going to San Antonio," I replied. "We're going to Houston."

"No," he said, "we're going to San Antonio. Isn't that where you wanted to go?" He reached up to push the attendant button to let them know I was on the wrong flight, when I grabbed his hand.

"No!" I said. "I'm a Southwest employee, and I *can't* delay this flight!"

I ended up flying to Houston via San Antonio. That experience changed my perspective of people getting on the wrong flight.

## *Principle #5:*
## Continually foster a fun environment.

As you can imagine, employees who work at Southwest Airlines walk into a fresh "bag of goodies" every day. Fun and excitement permeate the air, and they never know who will be "up to" what.

When I arrived at the office one day, I noticed puppy paw prints glued to the floor. Curious, I followed the path, which led to a "puppy shower" for the lone male employee in a department of 10. He had just adopted a puppy, and his coworkers wanted to honor him with a puppy shower because he had so faithfully attended all of their baby and wedding showers over the years!

Halloween is a *huge* event at Southwest Airlines. In the Marketing Department, we always invited customers to the home office to observe our Halloween celebration. Every station and every face was decorated!

One Halloween, my group decided to go dressed as a pajama party. I came in a fuzzy pink robe and slippers with pink rollers in my hair and cold cream on my face. I was traipsing through the airport on my daily commute when one customer looked at her husband and said, "Man, she must have *really* gotten up late!"

This "casual wear" occasionally brought unique feedback from our customers. We had just moved into new offices in the heart of Houston's business district, and I was in the elevator one day going to my office when a gentleman with another firm said, "You guys have made my life very, very difficult."

"Why?" I asked him, ready to right any wrong we may have inflicted on a customer.

"Because my employees have watched all of you go up and down in these elevators, laughing and having fun, dressed in these fun clothes and now they want to go casual!"

I celebrated my 50th birthday while working at Southwest, and when I walked into the office that day, the entire department was dressed in '50s costumes! One of the mechanics was a really good Elvis impersonator and coworkers asked him to perform. Then they all did a little skit and sang "50 Candles." As busy as we all were, they still felt my half-century mark was important enough to celebrate!

When I left Southwest, my coworkers created a comic strip of my life there, calling it "Hurricane Lorraine." It included all the fun stories (the wrong flight to San Antonio, etc.). This will always serve as a precious reminder that I found "the kid in me" at Southwest Airlines!

# *Loyalty* #**5**
# Lesson

## Find the Kid in Everyone

## *Loyalty*Principles

#1 | Let your company's advertising reflect the fun in your company culture.

#2 | Incorporate fun in employee training.

#3 | Empower your employees to have fun in communicating with your customers!

#4 | Hire people who can laugh at themselves.

#5 | Continually foster a fun environment.

# *Loyalty* #**6**
## Lesson

## Do More with Less

$I$ had just completed a presentation to an MBA class at the University of Houston about the culture at Southwest Airlines. My son Landon, who was attending classes there at the time, was with me and I was pleased to share the unique and wonderful stories about Southwest Airlines at my alma mater.

"Well, what did you think about the presentation?" I asked Landon as we left. "Wow! You guys sure have a lot of fun there," he said. "But I don't know when you work!"

Southwest Airlines is not *just* about having fun. It is about very, very hard work and dedication, but when people are having fun on their jobs, they will give exactly that!

To emphasize that point, I'm including a chapter about the incredible diligence and dedication of the Southwest Airlines employees. Yes, fun is fostered and treasured there but on the other side of the coin, the company expects its employees to work hard – very hard! The fun and games and celebrations are all actually part of a larger strategy to encourage employees to work harder.

Remember, the employees take ownership in the company because they actually are owners through the company's remarkable profit-sharing plan. As you know, no one works harder to make a business successful than its owners. So, again, we see a two-sided coin: The company's continued success requires hard work, but because the employees have a vested interest in making the company successful, they *willingly* work hard. As a result, Southwest Airlines has a very disciplined workforce. From frontline people to top management, the first principle involved in preserving a dedicated workforce is recognized and held fast:

## *Principle #1:*
## Insist your employees live by a "doing more with less" philosophy.

The "doing more with less" message is repeated daily at Southwest Airlines and employees hear it from their first day on the job. *Everyone*, company wide, is expected to work hard and accomplish all they can while spending the least they can.

For example, Southwest's planes are in the air more hours than its competitors' and its jetways are used more than most. The leaders and employees at Southwest look at it this way: Those are fixed assets and the company is going to pay for them whether they are used one time or 10 times a day. High usage of the company's facilities and assets is key to profitability.

It's always a good investment for your organization to keep your employees busy, to encourage them to do more with less. Why? Because they feel not only needed but of increased value to the organization. Keeping them busy allows little time for extracurricular – and unproductive – activities. For instance, one study found when a government agency's employees were at their computers, they were spending 50 percent of that time buying personal items online, playing online games or sending personal e-mail to family and friends.

You only have to spend a few minutes at any airport Southwest serves to see how busy its employees are kept. The time it takes to "turn" an airplane at a gate has a tremendous effect on the bottom line. Southwest does this better than any other airline – because, unlike the government agency, Southwest's employees don't have time to do personal business on company time. They have too much to do, too many passengers to serve.

In order to help new customers understand our flight philosophy, we would often bring them to the airport to watch the incredible phenomenon of getting a plane turned around in 20 minutes or less. We encouraged them to clock the time – from the moment the aircraft pulled up to the gate until it departed, explaining all the tasks required to turn the plane around … and the customers were always amazed as they watched the various employee groups working together to accomplish such a feat!

Southwest Airlines has fewer employees per aircraft than any other airline. The reason that works, of course, is the *productivity* of its workforce. We were renowned among our competitors for having the hardest working people in the industry.

In keeping with its "doing more with less" philosophy, Southwest does not build fancy, high-cost terminals and facilities. In fact, many of its stations operate in unique and difficult physical environments. For example, Hobby Airport in Houston operates with a split concourse. When weather dictates flight and gate changes, people and luggage must be moved from one concourse to another (and must pass through another security checkpoint).

In keeping with the philosophy of doing more with less at Southwest, there are no fancy offices at the headquarters building in Dallas. All offices are about the same size and there is very little, if any, professional decorating because that is a frill the leaders at Southwest choose not to afford. (Hence, the employees are given the freedom to decorate their offices and cubicles as they wish. Remember the hanging cow?)

If employees wanted frills, they would conduct a fundraiser to accomplish their goals. The Provisioning Department in Houston had a basketball hoop and a ping-pong table in the middle of a warehouse, both paid for by fundraisers carried out by the employees. In some stations, one work group might conduct a fundraiser to buy break room amenities for another work group.

Because most everyone is a team player and wants to do whatever it takes to make the company successful, it is not unusual to see pilots inside the aircraft crossing the seatbelts and picking up trash after the passengers deplane – or retrieving strollers for parents from the ramp agents and helping out with luggage.

Flight attendants might help with luggage after their jobs are done inside the aircraft, as well. Even "non-rev" employees flying on the fourth seat with the flight attendants will pitch in and help clean the plane or serve peanuts during the flight. The whole atmosphere is one of teamwork – everyone helping get the job done!

It was understood by all department leaders that when unusual circumstances, such as snowstorms, floods, or some other type of bad weather, hit a station, it was all hands on deck to help. We would help people in wheelchairs, play gate games, tag customers bags or do whatever else was needed at the time. During the holidays – especially Thanksgiving and Christmas – most departments would provide a list of employees willing to volunteer at the terminals during the rush.

I learned, early on, how unique our philosophy of working hard and doing more with less really was. The Marketing Department in Houston networked with sales reps from other airlines at a monthly luncheon. I attended one of these luncheons as a fairly new employee and was talking to my counterpart at another airline. "I bet you guys are really, really busy," I said. "I notice you have flights out of Intercontinental Airport in Houston. How many flights a day are your sales reps responsible for marketing?"

"Oh," the counterpart replied, "We have nine flights a day!"

"Really?" I said. "How many employees?"

"Forty or 50," he estimated.

"How many people are in your Marketing and Sales Department?" I asked.

"About 25 or 30," he replied.

Yes, it was very different at Southwest. At that time we had over 100 flights a day out of Houston's Hobby Airport and our little team of nine marketing reps was responsible for overseeing the marketing for all flights out of Houston, Nashville, Birmingham, New Orleans, Harlingen, Corpus Christi and San Antonio. I realized, then and there, we at Southwest were doing so much more with so much less – and we were doing it very well!

Admittedly, few positions at Southwest were the usual 8-to-5 jobs. It's not that we worked 24 hours a day, mind you, but we did work hard … and smart. If there was a need, people jumped to get it done – whether they were on break or lunch or in another department or about to leave for the day – and they left only when the task was complete.

Occasionally, some people had to work longer hours due to extenuating circumstances. During bad weather, employees were required to work extra shifts to cover the operation. Usually the newer employees were "juniored" and required to stay, but for the most part, however, Southwest's employees all realized the importance of keeping the planes flying on time and the entire workforce was dedicated to that goal – whatever that took.

Safety is the number one priority at Southwest. Shortcutting procedures are ***never*** condoned, no matter how they may affect the bottom line. Southwest empowers its employees to do the *right thing*.

The captain of a plane has the freedom to ground the aircraft if, in his or her opinion, the safety of its passengers requires grounding – and the pilot is never punished for doing the right thing. To the contrary, the company supports and applauds the pilot's diligence in safeguarding the safety of the passengers, even if the flight is delayed.

Without a doubt, the airline industry is a tough business. Every day is different and employees are trained to always be prepared for the unexpected: weather challenges, mechanical failures, etc.

During bad weather anywhere in an airline's system, two issues surface at its major airports: getting planes in and getting planes out. Bad weather on a Friday evening can be especially harrowing. The planes are usually completely booked with people winding up their workweek and anxious to go home. As the planes start backing up and more and more people arrive, it can get very chaotic.

On one such Friday evening, there were hundreds of people in the gate area as I prepared to take my regular flight from Dallas to Houston. There was barely room to move and people had difficulty getting to the ticket counter for their boarding passes when their names were called.

I watched the Southwest customer service agents throughout the evening, extremely impressed with the way they remained calm and communicated with the customers – even when they had bad news to share (like, "Ladies and gentlemen, the plane has not yet left Oklahoma City.").

Southwest's agents know it is always better to communicate with the customers, even when the news is bad, and while there were many frustrated customers that evening, none became irate.

I watched as the customer service agents answered the same questions asked by different customers throughout the evening. I knew they must be very tired and frustrated, but they never showed it. Within three hours, they had cleared the entire terminal.

In the process, they chose to keep people informed – and even managed to infuse a little humor throughout the evening. People couldn't hear their names called because of the noise of the crowd, so the agents would say to the people closest to the counter, "Would you please tap your neighbor on the shoulder and ask if he is Mr. Brown? We need Mr. Brown to come to the counter." They even said at one point, "Would someone please walk into the bar and see if Mr. Brown is in there?"

When the rubber hits the road – like that night in Dallas – they must be consummate team players in order to keep the entire team (the "orchestra") synchronized and moving in the right direction. When the unexpected happens, everyone on the team has to be willing to stay and work hard until the job is done.

## Principle #2:
## Maintain tough love with your employees, but with a huge heart.

As I've said, not everyone made it at Southwest Airlines. Not everyone was able – or willing – to give the kind of diligence and dedication required. Even though we were very successful in attracting and hiring the right people, there were a few who just never could settle into the Southwest "mold."

Maintaining the culture is so *important* at Southwest a full 20 percent of *all* performance reviews count toward an evaluation of the person's "Southwest spirit."

Sounds strange? Absolutely – because the "Southwest spirit" is not a definable characteristic – but it is measurable. Although it meant different things to different people in the different departments, everyone recognized it when they saw it. Some defined it as what employees did for their fellow employees. Some thought it was what employees did for the company. Others thought it pertained to the kind of attitude. Still others thought it had to do with whether the employees went "above and beyond."

I was a participant in a training class in which we attempted to define the "Southwest spirit." It was an impossible task. We never reached a conclusion. We were all throwing out certain *attributes* of "Southwest spirit" (company parties, celebrations, birthday recognition, special events, the culture, etc.), but we could not come up with an all-encompassing definition.

Finally, a very frustrated dispatcher spoke up. "You guys just don't get it! For me, "Southwest spirit" is my being here when I am needed and my giving *150 percent of myself when I am here*. But don't expect me to come to your holiday parties or after-hours events because I want to go home and be with my family."

When I transferred into the People Department, part of my job description entailed performing exit interviews with employees who were leaving the company – either of their own volition or the company's. I dreaded it! Southwest Airlines was one giant heart, and people there loved one another so much, I thought I would hate that part of my job.

Much to my delight, it turned out to be one of the most valuable contributions I made at Southwest! I found I was able to give people an opportunity to add closure to their experience at Southwest. I always had a director from the employee's department attend the exit interview, but my goals were:

- to listen objectively to what the employees had to say and give them a fair opportunity to express their thoughts about the company, their department and the event or events leading to their termination or decision to leave the company

- to help them become accountable about what had happened

- to help the employees attain closure and move on with their lives

We occasionally found that the employee should not have been terminated. In those rare cases, we had to go back and revisit the entire situation, usually finding extenuating circumstances in the employee's life. The individual may have been going through a tremendously difficult personal upheaval, and if this information had been shared with the supervisor, it would have made a difference in the decision to terminate.

We also found that sometimes an employee with a good attitude just needed to be moved to another department to accommodate his or her needs.

I occasionally even ran across letters from leaders who stated they hated to terminate the employee, but they felt they had no choice. Then they would proceed to make a case for the employee's future eligibility for rehire!

A few months before I left the company, we had a situation in which a young man hit and damaged an aircraft with a piece of equipment. At Southwest Airlines, that is a very serious offense and usually, after investigation, results in dismissal. His leader had marked his personnel file "ineligible for rehire."

The young man showed up at the exit interview with a three-page letter in which he explained he was not trying to get his job back. He knew what he had done was wrong. His reason for requesting an exit interview was that he just wanted to say he was very sorry and did not want us to think badly of him.

It was an incredible letter, and it got our attention. We went back to the leader and presented our case on his behalf. We knew others we had rehired had become our strongest advocates. We felt that he would be a real asset to the company if he were allowed to reapply in one year. His status was changed to "eligible for rehire in one year."

## *Principle #3:*
## Measure everything!
In spite of the fun and fluff, Southwest Airlines is actually one of

the most disciplined companies around. Operationally, everything is measured and the three most important metrics are those kept by the Department of Transportation:

- On-time performance

- Baggage lost

- Customer complaints

Anytime an airplane is late, it gets logged to the work group responsible. It may have been because of a mechanical issue, the flight crew may not have gotten things together or operations may not have had the paperwork ready.

With over 2,000 flights a day, it is an enormous task to log all the metrics, but those metrics are taken very seriously at Southwest Airlines. Departments or stations with outstanding metrics are recognized and those with high numbers logged against them are scrutinized to determine the problems:

- Is there something wrong with the process?

- Was the manpower coverage per shift adequate?

- Were there equipment problems?

- Were there circumstances beyond the control of the teams involved?

There is often a fine line between keeping costs low and making wrong decisions that delay planes. For example, a station manager may decide not to pay overtime in order to keep down the costs, but the current staff may not be able to handle the load, which makes the planes late.

Southwest's "Mom Committee" – made up of senior executives – is probably the airline's most unique measure, and they meet daily to review aircraft delays from the previous day. The metric they apply to every delay is, "If my mom had been on that plane, how would I have felt about the way the situation was handled?" It is a very effective way to apply Southwest's "heart" to its operational metrics.

Metrics are utilized in every department. In the Marketing Department, market share is measured and compared to other airlines. In the People Department, the metric is cost per hire. Leaders are measured in large part by the morale of their groups.

Group morale is extremely visible and, because of the open-door policy at Southwest, employees have the freedom to go over their leaders' heads if they can't achieve resolution on an issue.

Do volatile situations ever occur among Southwest Airlines employees? Very occasionally, but when they do, the situations are always addressed immediately and not allowed to fester. Overall, the level of teamwork and harmony is *much* higher at Southwest than at other companies.

A very common and effective metric, of course, is the budget. At Southwest, we were continually pumped with the mindset that bad times were just around the corner. We treated good times as if they were bad times. I was hired in 1989, which happened to be one of Southwest's most profitable years and remember thinking, "Oh good, now I can get a new computer."

That was not the case. Every year we were told to keep our budgets flat. We were asked to filter everything through the metric "Is it a nice-to or a have-to?" We always looked for a return on investment.

The People Department needed a new Applicant Tracking System for years but we kept putting it off because of the expense. We finally reached the point where we absolutely had to have one and put together a proposal to buy one – the system had become a definite "have-to-have."

The University for People employees who traveled around the system could have used laptop computers years before they actually got one. One? Yes, it was a roving laptop for the person who was traveling.

As a team, we had brainstormed the issue: "I go to a ticket counter computer no one is using and ask an agent to sign me in. I can get to my e-mail any time I need to," said one employee. "I walk into the station manager's office and ask if I can use an empty computer," another said. Issue resolved.

How do Southwest's employees feel about these restraints? Remember, they are part owners of the company through the profit-sharing plan. It suits them just fine!

*Loyalty* **#6**
**Lesson**

## Do More with Less

# *Loyalty*Principles

*#1* Insist your employees live by a "doing more with less" philosophy.

*#2* Maintain tough love with your employees, but with a huge heart.

*#3* Measure everything!

# Loyalty Lesson #7

# Luv 'Em in Tough Times

"**G**o home early, and have your two sons and your husband dressed and ready to go by three o'clock," I was instructed.

My husband had been ill with cancer for over two years and everyone in the Marketing Department in Houston – where I worked at the time – and elsewhere across the system had provided *incredible* support. Baskets of cards from people across the company dotted the landscape inside my home and many had even *given me their vacation days* so I could spend time with my husband at the hospital!

At three o'clock sharp, a huge black limousine pulled up in front of our home and the *entire* staff from my office piled out! Excitedly, they explained that they were sending me and my family to dinner at a five-star restaurant and then to see a performance of *A Christmas Carol*. It was the middle of December, and we had a marvelous family evening – one I will never forget. It would also be the last meal my husband was able to eat. He passed away just a few weeks later.

This is one of thousands of equally generous gestures from my doting, loving Southwest Airlines family and a perfect example of how to apply the first principle I want to address in this chapter:

## *Principle #1:*
## Take very good care of your people when they are going through difficult times *personally*.

In Loyalty Lesson #4, we discussed the concept of recognizing and appreciating your employees. At Southwest Airlines, this doesn't stop with the good times. You see, the people at Southwest Airlines are just as careful to apply the lesson of "luv 'em in tough times" when their employees are experiencing *bad* times in their personal lives, too.

At one point in my husband's illness, I realized that his insurance policy's 20 percent co-payment – which came out of our pockets – would soon overtake us with the catastrophic medical bills we were paying, and I had not added him to my policy at Southwest.

During the annual enrollment period that year, I met with the director of the Benefits Department and told her my dilemma. "Go ahead and add him now," she said. "Yes, his illness will be considered a pre-existing condition, but after one year, our insurance will pay that other 20 percent retroactively."

He lived one year and two weeks beyond that conversation, and Southwest's insurance did indeed pick up the slack, retroactive to the beginning of his illness.

My amazement was not that the insurance paid the money, but that the person at Southwest *advised me* to add my husband to the policy – knowing that, as a self-insured company, Southwest Airlines would be out a lot of money. In other words, supporting a hurting employee was more important than saving money for the company.

Several months before my husband died, the Houston Astros asked Southwest to select someone to throw out the first pitch of the season. Normally, this honor would have gone to one of Southwest's top customers. However, in a wonderful gesture of kindness and support, they allowed my husband to throw out the first pitch on that occasion. I'll never forget the grin on his face as he wound around and pitched the ball to the catcher with the whole stadium cheering.

That year was a tough one for me. In October, just three months before my husband died, my mother passed away very unexpectedly. The morning of the funeral, my entire office in Houston and many from the Marketing Department in Dallas cleaned my house to get it prepared for guests, brought in food, prepared and organized everything for the gathering at my home after the funeral, cleaned up afterwards, and then disappeared!

It was a marvelous show of love and support when I needed it the most.

There is an amazing infrastructure in place at Southwest to keep its employees informed when one of their own is going through a difficult time. Leaders are trained early on to keep this important support network informed of good or bad events in their employees' lives through e-mail, and then to send updates as things progress.

The e-mails also go to the leader's entire group and include the employee's home address so the members of the team can send cards or offer additional support.

A few months ago, I was looking for a coworker who was scheduled to help me work on a project that morning. I discovered she had not yet arrived at the office because she had spent the night in the emergency room at the hospital in support of another coworker.

One of my managers had been out for foot surgery for several weeks, and to give her a boost and show her she was missed, our group picked up food from a local restaurant, took it to her home and had a nice lunch with her. She thanked us for keeping her in the loop and making her feel like she was still part of the team.

Southwest employees definitely take care of their own. On any given day, you'll find some kind of fundraiser going on for an employee who is going through difficult times.

In addition to the fundraisers, there is also a Catastrophic Assistance Fund, subsidized 100 percent by the employees of Southwest Airlines through payroll deductions. New hires are given the opportunity to pledge whatever amount they want to go into this fund each pay period.

There is a board of Southwest employees that processes the requests, and to date, approximately $5 million has been given to those who have gone through calamitous events in their lives.

Funds have been provided for an employee whose spouse lost his/her job and they were about to lose their house because they couldn't make the payments. They've also been given to an employee whose child developed a catastrophic illness that required one parent to quit his/her job and stay home with the child, and they were struggling financially. Sometimes it's for an employee whose home was hit by a tornado or damaged in a hurricane.

At Southwest Airlines, employees are accepted and treated as "whole people." Its leaders realize their employees' personal lives cannot be separated from their work lives, nor do they want that to happen. Personal challenges affect people, and Southwest's leaders realize it is unreasonable to expect people to stifle life's difficult circumstances for the sake of their jobs.

## *Principle #2:*
## Take very good care of your people when *the company* is going through difficult times.

The company is not immune to the bad times, either. However, when those times do come, Southwest's leaders ask, "How can we best deliver the message and bring the least negative impact to our people?"

When I was in the People Department, it became necessary to close three reservations centers, consolidating them into the remaining six. The new "ticketless travel" had allowed customers to begin making reservations online instead of calling the centers.

During the first several years of this paradigm shift, the company vigorously avoided the consolidation by shifting schedules, eliminating overtime, etc. Through all of its difficult times,

Southwest had never furloughed its employees and it was determined not to this time, either.

When the consolidation became inevitable, every employee at all three centers was offered the opportunity to transfer to another center, and if they had chosen to do so, every single one of them would have had jobs.

The executive leaders at Southwest Airlines understood that when there was a tough assignment to be done, they were the ones to do it. They brought the leaders from the three centers into the headquarters office, gave them the message and helped them work through all of their emotions so they could go back and help their people.

Next, the responsible executive vice president of the company, the vice president of the Reservations Department and senior directors personally went to each center to deliver the message to the people.

For weeks prior to the announcement of the consolidation, we had been in closed-door meetings in the People Department, creating a plan to help the people involved. Our number one priority was to help the affected employees develop skills and resumes that would make them competitive in the marketplace.

We put together a three-week training program that included resume writing, how to find a job on the Internet, interviewing skills and computer skills, including all of the components of the Microsoft Office package. In addition, we offered an opportunity to enroll in over 300 online classes – free of charge – paid for by Southwest Airlines.

Because of Southwest's reputation for hiring good people and providing excellent training, when news of the consolidation went public, we were inundated with calls from other companies wanting to hire our people. We also partnered with the communities to do what we called a "reverse job fair," scheduling a day in each of the three locations for other companies to come and interview our people.

To be sure our employees were prepared for the interviews, we spent several weeks prior to the job fairs, conducting training classes daily from 6:00 a.m. to 2:00 a.m. the next morning to accommodate the various shifts. Many of these people had never worked anywhere other than for Southwest Airlines and were experiencing a tremendous amount of fear about going to other jobs "out there."

At that point, I realized a downside to pulling people into the Southwest Airlines culture so effectively: They couldn't see how they could be successful on the outside. We had done such a good job of drawing them into the culture, they didn't know how to leave.

To assist in the transition, we offered a change management class to help them work through the process, and we gave them our phone numbers so they could call us for support.

Interestingly, a big issue with many of them was whether they were going to have a center-closing party. They did, of course. Because we had bonded with them so much during the process, those of us who conducted training classes went back to attend the parties and send them off to start the next chapter in their lives.

Southwest gave their employees a three-month advance warning *plus* all the other benefits to help them cope. How could we not?

They were good people who had given of themselves above and beyond for the company.

Close to 30 percent of the approximately 1,900 employees involved in the consolidation opted for transfers to other reservations centers and also received the care and assistance necessary for a successful transfer. Employees at their new job locations welcomed them with open arms. Many "adopted" the transferring employees, sending them packets of information about the city, inviting them to stay with them, and helping them look for housing.

One of the best examples of a company supporting its employees through hard times was Southwest's response following 9/11. When that horrific event occurred, all airplanes were grounded and within hours, all the other airlines began talking about furloughs and layoffs, but Southwest immediately came out with a message, reassuring its employees there would be no layoffs and pledging to keep everyone in the loop as much as possible about plans for making it through this catastrophe.

One of the executive officers' first steps was a voluntary commitment to forfeit their pay through the end of the year. No layoffs and officers forfeiting their pay was amazing enough, but within two weeks, another astonishing announcement was made. Southwest intended to fund their profit-sharing plan in October as usual.

As a result of 9/11, many departments had little to do, but rather than laying people off, Southwest got creative. They developed a program called "Loan Your Luv" where they created an in-house temporary staffing agency that loaned employees to different departments finding themselves suddenly overwhelmed – like

Refunds, Ticketing and Customer Service, which were all fielding thousands of phone calls from customers.

One exception to the hiring freeze that immediately followed 9/11 was the large number of customer service agents we hired to facilitate the increased airport screening requirements. When the federal government formed the Transportation Security Administration (TSA) and brought in its own people to do the security screening several months later, we were left with an overabundance of employees.

As was its tradition, Southwest Airlines chose not to lay off any of its people. Actually, we thought normal attrition would take care of the problem, but as it turned out, very few companies were hiring in the years after 9/11, so none of our people left.

Again, Southwest took the positive approach and created a program called Freedom '04, which was a totally voluntary initiative offering people the opportunity to leave the company *with insurance, flight benefits and a cash incentive*! The new program was enticing enough to several hundred people – including myself – who took advantage of that incredible opportunity.

In conjunction with Freedom '04, we introduced another program – "Going Where We Are Growing" – offering employees in overstaffed areas the opportunity to transfer to other locations that were understaffed, and we also created an internal drive to fill our next class of flight attendants.

There were employees at Southwest who wanted to be flight attendants for years, and they jumped at the chance – especially when we told them that if they failed because of poor grades, they could return to their former positions. Through this program, we were able to fill two classes of 140 each with people from all areas of the company.

Southwest Airlines does many things well. But one of the things it does *best* is taking care of its people – in the bad times, as well as the good.

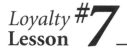

*Loyalty* **Lesson** **#7** _____

## Luv 'Em in Tough Times

# *Loyalty*Principles

*#1* | Take very good care of your people when they are going through difficult times *personally.*

*#2* | Take very good care of your people when *the company* is going through difficult times.

*Loyalty*
**Lesson** **#8**

# Do What's Right

*I* attended a meeting in Dallas to discuss the department's sales goals for the coming year. Our team had worked very hard and had exceeded all of our goals for the current year, but the goals set by my leaders for the next year were almost double. It seemed an impossible objective.

I tried to express my concerns in the meeting to no avail. I rarely got upset at my job with Southwest Airlines, but when I left the meeting to fly back to Houston, I was frustrated.

My director contacted me the next day. He had noticed my uncharacteristically subdued behavior in the meeting and was concerned enough to call. After a few minutes of listening to my frustrations, he said, "Why don't we sit down and talk about this. I'll be in Houston on Friday."

By the time he arrived, I had gathered all my sales data to prove my point and the director spent *three hours* going over the material.

"You know what, you are absolutely right, Lorraine," he finally admitted, recognizing the goals he had established were unreasonable and unfair. He apologized, rescinded the sales goals back to a realistic objective and then took the whole group to lunch.

My director had just demonstrated the first principle in Southwest Airlines' leadership philosophy:

## *Principle #1:*
## Choose leaders who aren't afraid to do what they think is right.

At Southwest, everyone deserves a good leader and being a good leader is not necessarily having an Ivy League education or having read all the right books. At Southwest, a good leader is someone who not only has good business sense, but also possesses *common sense*. A good leader knows how to *do the right thing* when making good business decisions.

"*Who you work for is as important as what you do*" is a closely held belief at Southwest Airlines. In other words, the employees choose their leaders as carefully as they select their jobs. Once employees find leaders for whom they enjoy working – with whom they "fit" – they stay with them.

At one point, Southwest was looking for a new vice president for the People Department, and we were temporarily assigned to report to one of the executive vice presidents of the company who was responsible for selecting the next vice president.

Because of the company's open-door policy, I was able to explain to the executive VP how fortunate I had been to have excellent leaders during my 10-year career at Southwest and that I wanted to share my hopes about the traits the leader chosen for this position would possess. We had a frank discussion as I described the leader for whom I would enjoy working.

As it turned out, the executive VP selected a wonderful vice president.

Early on, leaders are also taught the three most important phrases they need to know:

- I don't know

- I messed up

- Please help me

Some business theories espouse the philosophy that "the business of business is business." At Southwest Airlines, leaders are taught that "the business of any business is *people*, in the beginning and in the end." Consequently, employees see leaders who care about and support their people. Most realize their leaders' philosophy is, "I'll trust you until I know I can't," as opposed to the theory of, "I won't trust you until I know I can."

They also watch leaders use their common sense and do the *right* thing, even when it may stretch the company's established guidelines.

## *Principle #2:*
## Empower your people to "do the right thing" versus "do what's right by the book."

Leaders at Southwest are given a great deal of latitude – because they are good people – and they are trusted. They also are *empowered* to make decisions based on common sense. They are not expected to just follow a lot of rules and ignore the right thing to do when it comes to the best interest of their employees or their customers. Let me give you an example:

> A particular station had been charged with an unusually high number of delayed flights. Remember the metrics used at Southwest Airlines and the fact that every time a plane was late, those metrics pinpointed the work group responsible for the delay? In this instance, a new employee just happened to be on duty at one of the gates and she had been drilled about the importance of not delaying the flights.

> Taking that direction to heart, the Employee "pushed" (an airline operational phrase used for closing the aircraft door and releasing the aircraft to taxi) the plane on time, despite the fact that a paraplegic was waiting to board the aircraft. The employee determined that it would delay the plane too much to board the disabled passenger and she made the decision to prioritize the on-time departure over customer service.

> The paraplegic customer had to wait in the terminal for hours for the next flight!

We used that example in our training classes as an example of what *not* to do! In that case, following the rules was not the best decision. That particular delay on the books would have been forgiven had the employee held the plane. Why? Because it would have been the right thing to do.

Employees at every level at Southwest were empowered to use common sense, do the right thing and bring ideas to the table.

Years ago, I had a friend at Hobby Airport who was a ticket agent. We were flying together one day – which just happened to be Boss' Day – and she was reading a newspaper. "Wouldn't it be neat," she said, "if all of our employees could band together next year and buy a Boss' Day ad for Herb Kelleher?"

I thought it was a marvelous idea.

Several months later, I called the director of advertising and shared my friend's suggestion. "I think this is a really good idea," she said.

The advertising department, in turn, got in touch with my friend who originally had the idea, and ultimately, the Culture Committee became involved in raising the money.

When the full-page ad ran in *USA Today* on Boss' Day of the next year, the entire $60,000 had been paid for by the employees of Southwest Airlines, and the company didn't have to spend a dime!

We also had planned a giant "unveiling" ceremony for Herb on Boss' Day and because of the stories in the media, we had to arrange for someone to "steal" the newspaper off Herb's front porch that morning so he wouldn't read about it and spoil the surprise!

The ad generated a tremendous amount of PR mileage and the story about what the employees had done for Herb on Boss' Day made headline news all over the country.

✦   ✦   ✦

After 9/11, the airline industry began changing.

Every day there were at least 10 to 15 new security directives. Communicating them to all the right people became a nightmare. In the chaos and confusion that followed, we suddenly realized our employees were coming up with their own solutions to all the craziness and taking responsibility for resolving many of the problems that were surfacing. Because they knew the legal parameters within which they had to work, they felt sufficiently empowered to make common sense decisions and do the right thing.

When we realized our customers were having to wait in the long lines and endure all the changes after 9/11, we wanted to come up with solutions that would help make their travel experiences easier.

Rather than trying to figure out the solutions by ourselves, we formed focus groups across the system, allowing frontline people who were already executing many solutions themselves to tell us what was working.

After collecting these ideas, the leaders then came back and put them in the form of directives to all employees. We didn't need to hire high-priced consultants – we had over 31,000 creative consultants to guide us. All Southwest had to do was trust its employees – and listen.

## *Principle #3:*
## Train your leaders to spend time getting to know their people.

It's difficult for someone from the "outside" who has not been immersed in the Southwest culture to come in and hit the mark as a successful leader.

New leaders at Southwest are told, "Don't try to learn your job. Your first priority is to get to know your people!" This is one of the distinctions contributing to Southwest's enormous success.

When I taught leadership training classes at the University for People, we introduced an "ancient Japanese leadership style called "GTHOOYO," demonstrating a karate chop as we loudly chanted "Getoyo!"

Actually, this leadership style didn't originate in ancient Japan but, instead, was an acronym for "Get The Heck Out Of Your Office," better known as "Management by Walking Around" – an extremely important leadership technique at Southwest.

Southwest's executives came in the same doors and used the same elevators as everyone else, taking time to acknowledge people and say hello, taking the opportunity – whenever and wherever – to get to know their employees.

Years later, when I ran into my former director in the Marketing Department, he referred to the lesson he learned when he flew to Houston to discuss my concerns about the sales goals: Listen to the Employees.

The leaders at Southwest do listen to their people. Someone once told Herb Kelleher, "It is easier for frontline employees to get in to see you than it is for the directors of the company." Herb agreed because it is true.

The open-door policy at Southwest is not just lip service. It is a fact of life – from the top down. Open communication is promised to employees at all levels and those who want to see the executives or any other leader can do so simply by scheduling an appointment.

We've talked a lot about the fun, the family atmosphere, and the remarkable culture at Southwest Airlines. However, there are times when feathers get ruffled, and Southwest's executives have put into place as many safeguards as possible to ensure their people can be heard.

If employees are experiencing difficulty with their own leaders, they have the freedom to go above their heads to voice their dilemmas. These concerns are investigated and may even result in the dismissal of a leader if the negative morale in the group cannot be reversed after coaching and mentoring.

I mentioned earlier that one of the metrics used for leaders is the morale of their group. Leaders are accountable to that metric. While most work out the issues, the few who can't end up moving on. Most leaders at Southwest, however, have *exceptional* relationships with their people.

To establish relationships between leaders from the home office and employees in the field, Southwest initiated a program called "Leaders on Location" where, once a year, leaders from headquarters would visit each location in the system.

We would fly in one night and spend until 1:00 or 2:00 in the morning, visiting with the night shifts. We would bring in food and drinks and hang out in the break room, showing company videos and commercials, and just visiting.

Our goal was getting to know how things were going and whether the employees had everything they needed to do their jobs.

Then we would get up early the next morning and do the same thing with the pilot and flight attendant groups.

Later that day, we had a luncheon for supervisory and management personnel. In order for all leaders to attend, other locations would send in leaders to staff their stations. While there was still fun and games, the primary purpose of the luncheon was to share information about the company with the leaders (since we'd already done so in the break rooms with the employees) and answer any questions or address any issues they had.

Back at headquarters, we would report what we had learned from the employees in the field. Ultimately, the report was forwarded to the vice presidents of each department so they could follow up on the issues we found.

This was a great way for the company to stay on top of situations at individual stations, and we usually discovered the little things that, if left untended or unheard, caused people to decide their leaders didn't care. It also promoted the concept that Headquarters was a resource to them.

One executive program – the "Message to the Field" – was held annually in six of Southwest's largest locations. Employees were encouraged to come and hear a "state of the company" message, covering topics such as the state of the airline industry, and where the company was in accomplishing its mission and its goals for the next year.

The message also thanked the employees for their hard work and we made it a festive atmosphere, complete with drawings and prizes, attracting thousands of employees at each location.

All these events helped combat the "we vs. they" mentality (or the "Palace in Dallas" mentality, as it was called at Southwest) that tries to creep into any organization.

These events also put the leaders in direct communication with the employees in the field and promoted respect, friendship, and that sense of "family." Leaders were expected to attend as many events as possible – weekends, nights, or whenever – and they did so willingly.

## *Principle #4:*
## Live by the Golden Rule.

The bottom line of common sense is, simply, to live by the Golden Rule: Treat others like you want to be treated.

The "secret" to the phenomenal success at Southwest Airlines is that its people *live, breathe, eat and sleep* the Golden Rule. The leaders teach it to their employees and those employees hear it in their talk and see it in their walk. From the entry interview to the exit interview, the Golden Rule is a way of life.

At Southwest, people are celebrated as individuals and treated with respect. When the leaders live by the Golden Rule, they empower the employees to treat the customers the same way. That's why Southwest succeeded in building such a stellar reputation among its customers and why it is continually among the top performers in customer service ratings in its industry.

If you live by the Golden Rule, empowering your people to do the right thing, how can you go wrong?

*Loyalty* **Lesson** **#8**

# Do What's Right

# *Loyalty***Principles**

*#1* Choose leaders who aren't afraid to do what they think is right.

*#2* Empower your people to "do the right thing" versus "do what's right by the book."

*#3* Train your leaders to spend time getting to know their people.

*#4* Live by the Golden Rule.

## *Loyalty* Lesson #*9*

# Nurture the Corporate Family

W hen former President George Herbert Walker Bush moved back to Texas in 1992, Southwest's Marketing Department in Houston wanted to welcome him back to the city, so we sent him tickets to several of the sporting and cultural events we were sponsoring, along with a note: "Welcome home on behalf of the employees of Southwest Airlines." Then every couple of weeks we called his office to invite him and his staff to various events we were hosting throughout the city.

He never attended, but he always sent one or two staff members. Then came the unexpected call.

"I want to invite you and your entire marketing staff over to my office for breakfast," the former president said. "I would like to meet you."

We all went to his office for breakfast, of course!

That morning, former President Bush told how much it had meant for us to extend our hand of welcome to him and his staff. "What you didn't realize," he said, "is that many of my staff members came from Washington, D.C., to Houston for the first time, and they didn't know anyone. You graciously welcomed them, and they have had the best time going to your events in the community."

We had reached out to him, and as a result, former President George Bush had become a member of the Southwest Airlines family.

If you get nothing else out of this book, I hope you've become more aware of the importance of a strong sense of family within your corporate culture. The sense of belonging to a family is at the very heart of the Southwest Airlines culture – realizing you are part of something much larger than yourself – a team, a family that never stops loving and supporting, a family that has a lot of fun together but continually works together toward a focused goal.

*The camaraderie, loyalty and dedication that are built with this type of big-picture perspective will come back to your bottom line in a big way.*

The message of "we are family" is very, very strong at Southwest Airlines.

We knew that Herb Kelleher was coming to Houston from Dallas and a group of us wanted to be there to support him. When we arrived, Herb was deep in conversation with a group of some of the most prominent leaders in the Houston community.

Suddenly, Herb looked up, saw us and immediately said, "Excuse me. I have to leave. My family is here." He left the group and walked over to greet us. By doing so, he "shouted" a message to all who were watching: "My people at Southwest are my family, and they are important!"

That message prevails throughout the company.

In this chapter, I want to take the "family" concept one step further.

*The company's leaders and employees actually comprise only a fraction of the corporate family. There are other relationships pivotal to the success of any company.* In fact, without their contributions to your corporate family, you might as well close the doors and go home. I know that there would be no Southwest Airlines without the support and involvement of these special groups!

## Principle #1:
### Embrace your *community partners* as part of your corporate family.

At Southwest, the value placed on long-term relationships with community partners was validated some years ago by the "Good Neighbor Award." This special recognition is presented to a deserving community partner who has gone above and beyond for the benefit of Southwest Airlines.

At my 10-year anniversary banquet, the award was presented to an airport director who helped us bring service to his city in the midst of political turmoil. Another year, it was given to the president of the Harlingen, Texas, Chamber of Commerce for his continual support of the company, beginning with its earliest days.

Southwest's community partners are embraced as part of its family and *these relationships are carefully and meticulously cultivated and nurtured and are always cherished.*

Southwest's commitment to its relationships with community partners was made clear to me early in my career when I was responsible for the marketing efforts in an area that included the cities of Harlingen, Texas, and Nashville, Tennessee.

I was in the middle of a major marketing drive in Nashville and was looking for funds in my budget to move over to that initiative. We were well established in Harlingen and had been for years so I didn't see the need for allocating any marketing funds for that area.

Then I received a directive from the home office, asking us to stage a huge event in Harlingen. I knew we were not adding any flight service out of Harlingen, so I was having difficulty understanding why we would spend that kind of money on an established market. I called the vice president of marketing for clarification.

Earlier in this chapter, I mentioned the president of the Harlingen Chamber of Commerce was the one of the recipients of the Founder's Award. This year, Harlingen was celebrating an important milestone, and the president of the Chamber was spearheading the event. He had asked Southwest to co-host the event, and our executives immediately agreed – for a good reason.

In the beginning, when Southwest Airlines was struggling to get started, this gentleman had been one of its biggest advocates. Had it not been for him, Southwest's debut into the business world would have been even more difficult than it was.

The philosophy at Southwest has always been, "Never forget where you came from," and years later, when the Chamber president asked Southwest for this favor, our executives didn't hesitate. It was *the right thing to do.*

Another relationship Southwest Airlines has cultivated and cherished for many years is one with the Ronald McDonald House – the official charity for Southwest Airlines. Just recently, Southwest's newest signature aircraft, "The Spirit of Hope," was dedicated to the Ronald McDonald House program in celebration of its 30th birthday.

Southwest's involvement came about in 1983 through one of its pilots, Captain Dick East, who was introduced to the Ronald McDonald House program when his young daughter was diagnosed (and later lost her battle) with lymphoma.

The commitment to this program by Southwest employees has never dwindled. In fact, it has grown significantly over the years and, in the interim, Southwest's annual Ronald McDonald House Golf Classic has raised over $7 million.

## *Principle #2:*
## Cultivate relationships with your *industry partners and vendors* and bring them into the family.

My entire time with Southwest, I was always amazed at the way its employees worked to build relationships with the people with whom they did business. After 9/11, when the airline industry met difficult times, the government hired hundreds of thousands of TSA employees to implement security at the airports. In an industry defined by metrics, these people held enormous sway over our business. They could keep our planes from leaving on time by creating long lines at the security checkpoints or long delays in checking baggage.

The TSA employees simply did not understand the urgency with which Southwest's people worked. It didn't matter to them whether the planes turned in 20 minutes or not.

Systemwide, our frontline employees were becoming very frustrated because any interference on their part was seen as a power struggle, but during a visit to Oakland, I learned how our station there had resolved the issue.

*In typical Southwest style, they put together an initiative to build a relationship with the TSA by recognizing and appreciating the help its people were giving to Southwest Airlines.* They started bringing the TSA employees cookies or entire meals. As camaraderie was developed, the Southwest people explained their concerns and their needs to the TSA and made recommendations on how to make things flow easier and faster.

By embracing the TSA employees into the Southwest family, they gained their confidence and their respect, and the TSA people eventually became more cooperative with the Southwest team and began heeding their suggestions.

Along the same vein, the pilots at Southwest Airlines have a reputation for having excellent relationships with the FAA air traffic controllers. Why? Simply put, the pilots are nice to the controllers! They don't demand a particular routing or altitude. They make requests ... and not surprisingly, they often receive preferential treatment.

Again, it's the common sense approach.

When we negotiated with vendors at Southwest Airlines, we always looked for a win/win situation and we wanted it to be long term. If we really liked the vendor and felt he was doing everything in his power to give us the lowest price, we wanted to make sure he would still be in business for years down the road, so we would sometimes go back to that vendor and say, "Are you sure you can live with this price a year from now and still stay in business?"

It was a rather unique approach, but we wanted to make sure our vendors would be part of the Southwest family for years to come. After all, a "lifetime warranty" is really only a warranty for the lifetime of the company providing it.

## *Principle #3:*
## Recognize and embrace an *employee's family members* as part of your corporate family.

"Your families are now part of the Southwest family," we told our new employees because we realized their families were "loaning" their loved ones to us. We also knew there would be times when their families would be at home without them while they were hard at work for the company.

As a part of the Southwest family, the family members were often recognized by programs like those extending flight privileges to parents and dependents. Southwest's internal travel agency group – the Pass Bureau – hosted a "Travel Day" each year and the parents of new employees were flown to the home office to attend the fair and to learn, first hand, how to take full advantage of their travel benefits.

To show how successfully Southwest pulls employee's family members into its corporate family, let me share a story about my own father. He had just had surgery and was recovering in ICU, still under the influence of morphine.

Suddenly he reached up, grabbed my arm, and said, "Look! Look!"

"What?" I asked.

He pointed to a corner of the room where there were some really bright lights and said, "Look, they are over there filming a Southwest Airlines commercial. Look at the airplanes! Look at the people!"

Southwest Airlines was so deeply ingrained in him that he even hallucinated about it in ICU! We had a good laugh and, of course, he didn't remember a thing about it later.

"We are building a company for the future of our children" has been a mantra at Southwest Airlines since the beginning. Many employees take that mantra very seriously and believe they are building a company for which their children would be proud to work!

One of my coworkers in the People Department was one of the original employees of the company. A month before she retired last year, her daughter was hired. The baton had been passed – the ultimate example of the sense of pride instilled in the children of Southwest's employees.

## *Principle #4:*
## Your *customers* are a very important part of your corporate family.

These words appear at the bottom of every Southwest Airlines paycheck: "*This paycheck is made possible because of your customers.*" That simple statement says it all. Southwest – or any company – would not exist if it were not for its customers. There are, therefore, no relationships more important than those with customers.

At Southwest, every customer is treated with the utmost care. The company holds Customer Appreciation Days at its airports several times a year; and customers – like corporate partners, vendors, and employee family members – receive invitations to attend Southwest Airlines events.

On the shuttle returning to the headquarters from the airport one day, I was visiting with a couple of female pilots. They told me they had come to headquarters to help Customer Relations put together a response to a complaint they'd received about one of their flights. That particular flight not only had a female pilot and a female copilot, but also an all-female flight crew.

A customer had complained that the "flight attendants" never came out of the cockpit during the entire flight. They had to explain that the women in the cockpit were not flight attendants, but pilots.

We received another letter from a customer complaining about the words – "For Terminal Use Only" – on the backs of our wheelchairs at Hobby Airport. That letter made us realize we needed to change the wording. Sometimes it's not what you say, but how you say it! Our strategy at Southwest Airlines was to tap into the customer's emotional side and make them feel like part of our family. Apparently, we succeeded to a large degree – and this was never more evident than after 9/11, when many people in America were afraid to fly.

Most of our competitors were charging $100 or more to change or refund prepurchased tickets. At Southwest Airlines, however, we decided it was not the customers' fault 9/11 had happened and they should not be penalized for being afraid to fly.

We let our customers know that if they were afraid to fly because of 9/11 and wanted a refund, we would give them a full refund with no penalty. Now, if every customer who held a ticket had taken us up on our offer, we would have been in dire financial straits.

We were banking on our excellent relationships with our customers and the gamble paid off. Not all asked for a refund, but what was *even more incredible* – many of them sent back their tickets with a note saying something like: "Take this money and put it back into the company. At this point, you need it more than we do. We want you to be around years from now and don't want you to go bankrupt, so keep it!"

When the chips were down for Southwest Airlines, its customer family was right there to help.

This incredible company has given so much to so many. To the customer, it gives the freedom to fly affordably. To the community, it demonstrates the value of good corporate citizenry. To employees, it provides a great place to work … and a great place to learn, surrounded by family.

*Loyalty* **Lesson** **#9**

# Nurture the Corporate Family

# *Loyalty*Principles

*#1* | Embrace your *community partners* as part of your corporate family.

*#2* | Cultivate relationships with your *industry partners and vendors*, and bring them into the family.

*#3* | Recognize and embrace an *employee's family members* as part of your corporate family.

*#4* | Your *customers* are a very important part of your corporate family.

# Final Thoughts

Several months after I left Southwest Airlines, I flew to Alexandria, Virginia, and while I was there, I went to dinner with some business acquaintances. When someone in the group asked me what I did, I explained that I was in the process of writing a book about my 15 years with Southwest Airlines.

One of the men in our group had never flown Southwest and didn't know anything about the company, so I gave him an abbreviated version of the incredible culture, the fun, the camaraderie – everything I've talked about in this book.

When I finished, he asked the others at the table, "Have any of you ever flown Southwest?"

A couple of the ladies said they had.

"Is what she's saying true?" he asked.

"Oh, yes!" they agreed, "that and so much more!"

Now, more than ever, I am convinced the crucial difference between Southwest and other companies is its culture and its ability to breed such an incredible *loyal spirit* in its employees.

It's that call to arms, that spirit, that do-whatever-it-takes-to-keep-this-company-successful mentality that rallies its troops again and again to go above and beyond. The end result is a willingness to go to battle – and the determination to overcome – when the fight is on. It is a phenomenal thing to see.

I watched the troops rally the year Southwest ran a special for its senior-citizen customers. Not anticipating the overwhelming response – or the unique challenges, we ended up with anywhere from 25 to 40 wheelchair customers per flight. The employees gave their all to ensure flights went out on time. They just made it happen.

I saw it the year of Southwest Airlines' 25th anniversary, when we ran a $25 fare sale to any one-leg destination in Southwest's system. We were inundated with calls – so many that it momentarily shut down our phone system. Lines formed at airports beginning at about 4:00 a.m. and continued until 2:00 a.m. the next day.

Again, the wonderful, dedicated Southwest employees rose to the occasion and handled it beautifully. But, their feedback after the sales promotion? NEVER AGAIN!

As usual, the company listened and also let the employees know how much they appreciated everyone's efforts. The promotion had been very successful in enhancing the company's cash flow during the difficult economy that airlines were experiencing at that time.

Just after 9/11, Southwest's employees felt the company had done so much for us – by ensuring that we all kept our jobs and even funding our profit-sharing plan – we wanted to do something in return. The employees came up with an idea called "Pledge to Luv," where we pledged to give back to the company to help it through the tough times."

The company limited our giving to a maximum of two days pay because they knew some employees would have donated so much more and in doing so, may have put themselves in a financial bind!

When all planes were grounded on 9/11, we were forced to land some of our planes at airports that had no Southwest Airlines service. We had no ground crews at those locations and no one to help our customers find a place to go.

Many of them had no money with them, so the Southwest Airlines flight crews found hotels for them and, in some cases, used their own personal credit cards to pay for the passengers' rooms. One pilot even paid for train tickets to get customers home.

Our employees have always been willing to go that extra mile – or two or ten – for Southwest Airlines because they *know* that Southwest has always come through for them.

Someone once asked Herb Kelleher what accomplishment he was most proud of at Southwest Airlines. His response was, in essence, "In my 20 years as CEO, my primary goal and my principal accomplishment was to provide job security for all of the Southwest Airlines employees. When I say 'job security,' I am talking about providing the basic needs for our employees and their families – food, housing, clothing, education for their children, etc."

*Southwest Airlines is the only major airline in the United States that didn't ground any of its fleet, cut any of its flights or furlough any of its employees after 9/11.* This was while all the other large carriers were furloughing over 120,000 people! Southwest, which had never had to draw upon its "rainy day" credit before, was able to borrow $1 billion to keep its employees' futures secure and give them a paycheck, even when there was no guarantee that the airline would stay in business.

That's the example of commitment and loyal spirit that Southwest's employees witness daily and replicate.

It takes a tremendous amount of effort to maintain this level of buoyancy and loyalty. Employees also are reminded every day that the future of Southwest is in their hands, and leaders continually reminded all of us of Southwest's philosophy with these now-familiar slogans:

- The biggest challenge to your future is yourself

- Don't forget how you got here

- Remember the lessons that all the people coming before you have learned and taught

- Keep fares low and spirits high

- Remain altruistic

- Don't let success breed complacency

- Don't kill the golden goose

- Keep passing the torch

The lessons in loyalty I learned at Southwest Airlines have made an indelible imprint on my life, allowing me to walk away fully equipped to live a fulfilled life.

Now it's up to me. Will I be complacent and rest on my laurels, or will I choose to remember the lessons I learned from those who went before me?

I choose the latter … and I pass the torch to you.

# Lessons in Loyalty

### Hire Attitude – Train Skills

+ Make them want you before you want them.
+ Define the type of employee you want – then communicate it.
+ Tap into Marketing and PR Department strategies to enhance your recruiting efforts.
+ Make all employees recruiters.
+ Determine what's important to your company and design the interview around it.
+ Hire "nice" 'cause you can't train "nice."

### Immerse Everyone in the Culture Immediately

+ Establish an environment that helps new employees immediately identify with the company and makes them feel special.
+ Make orientation a celebration.
+ Train tough, but with heart.
+ It's smart to test the water to determine if new employees are really the right fit.

### Keep 'Em Learning

+ Consistently present unique training and learning opportunities to your people.
+ Capitalize on the expertise and experiences of your leaders in employee training.
+ Make training fun!
+ If you find a great book that can be used as a teaching tool, buy enough copies for your entire company.

### People Give as Good as They Get

+ Go to extreme measures to show your employees that they are highly valued.
+ Employee recognition and appreciation produce a very high yield (i.e., employees give as good as they get).
+ Employee recognition and appreciation can be achieved at a surprisingly low cost!

### Find the Kid in Everyone
✦ Let your company's advertising reflect the fun in your company culture.
✦ Incorporate fun in employee training.
✦ Empower your employees to have fun in communicating with your customers!
✦ Hire people who can laugh at themselves.
✦ Continually foster a fun environment.

### Do More with Less
✦ Insist your employees live by a "doing more with less" philosophy.
✦ Maintain tough love with your employees, but with a huge heart.
✦ Measure everything!

### Luv 'Em in Tough Times
✦ Take very good care of your people when they are going through difficult times *personally*.
✦ Take very good care of your people when *the company* is going through difficult times.

### Do What's Right
✦ Choose leaders who aren't afraid to do what they think is right.
✦ Empower your people to "do the right thing" versus "do what's right by the book."
✦ Train your leaders to spend time getting to know their people.
✦ Live by the Golden Rule.

### Nurture the Corporate Family
✦ Embrace your *community partners* as part of your corporate family.
✦ Cultivate relationships with your *industry partners and vendors* and bring them into the family.
✦ Recognize and embrace an *employee's family member* as part of your corporate family.
✦ Your *customers* are a very important part of your corporate family.

*Lessons in Loyalty Reminder Cards* are available at
www.CornerStoneLeadership.com

## ACKNOWLEDGEMENTS

Very little happens in life without help along the way.

Above all, I am blessed to have a family who has always stood by me. I know mom and pop would have been proud. To my sons, Sean and Landon, I wish a caring, nurturing work environment so you may experience the same joy. Jim, thanks for always being there.

To my extended Southwest Airlines family, I am indebted to you for the lessons learned. I was blessed to have many excellent mentors, leaders and coworkers at Southwest – Colleen Barrett, Herb Kelleher, Shell Stegall, Judy Haggard, Libby Sartain, Rita Bailey, Donna Conover, Beverly Carmichael, LuAnn Nevin, CJ Beutler, Fritz Petree, Anmarie Miller, Kris Stewart, Sherry Phelps, Jeannie Ebbighausen, Mark Wolfe, Ian Marshall, Tim Conners, Jennifer Taylor, Mary McMurtry, John Crisci … you make the world a better place – and you are setting the example others will follow.

To my "merry band of editors", Marcela Venturini, Catharina Mandic, Ginny West Case, Stephanie Concelman and Vicki Bronaugh who toughed it out with me, page by page, thank you. Additionally, I am grateful to: Tony Jeary, David Cottrell, Nonie Jobe, Alice Adams and Melissa Monogue for believing in the story and making it "so."

And to Rafael Rivas, my first business mentor now watching from above, who taught me that anything is possible.

# ABOUT THE AUTHOR

**Lorraine Grubbs-West**, president and CEO of Lessons in Loyalty, was a senior executive with Southwest Airlines for 15 years. Her career with Southwest included positions in marketing, employment and leadership development. Prior to Southwest, she was the founder of Aviation Charter International.

The mission of Lessons in Loyalty is to provide tools and resources for organizations to create a positive and productive culture. Her theme is that customer satisfaction begins with employee satisfaction because engaged, loyal employees create loyal customers.

Whether as a public presentation or an on-site consultation, Lorraine guides your organization through her proven lessons which emphasize putting people first, thereby creating loyal employees, faithful customers and a better bottom line.

Lorraine and her husband Jim live in Kemah, Texas, aboard their sailboat, the "Wandering Star."

Lorraine can be reached at 281-535-1334.
www.LessonsinLoyalty.com

# Four ways to bring the
## *Lessons in Loyalty*
# message to your team:

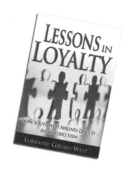

1. *Lessons in Loyalty PowerPoint® Presentation*

   Introduce and reinforce the *Lessons in Loyalty* to your organization with this complete and cost-effective companion presentation piece. All the main concepts and ideas in the book are reinforced in this professionally produced, downloadable **PowerPoint presentation with facilitator guide and notes**. Use the presentation for kick-off meetings, training sessions or as a follow-up development tool. **$79.95**

2. *Keynote Presentation*

   Invite author Lorraine Grubbs-West to deliver the *Lessons in Loyalty* message and inspire your team. Her presentation will set a solid foundation for improving your organization's success.

3. *Lessons in Loyalty Workshop*

   Facilitated by Lorraine Grubbs-West or a certified CornerStone Leadership instructor, this three- or six-hour workshop will reinforce the principles of *Lessons in Loyalty*.

4. *Lessons in Loyalty* **Reminder Card**

   4" x 5", laminated. **Pk/20    $19.95**

www.**CornerStoneLeadership**.com          **1.888.789.LEAD (5323)**

# Other CornerStone Leadership Resources

*Monday Morning Leadership* is David Cottrell's best-selling book. It offers unique encouragement and direction that will help you become a better manager, employee and person. $14.95

*Monday Morning Leadership for Women* provides insights and wisdom on how to deal with leadership issues that are unique to women. $14.95

*Monday Morning Communications* provides workable strategies to solve serious communications challenges. $14.95

*Sticking to It: The Art of Adherence* by Lee J. Colan reveals the secrets to success for high-achieving individuals and teams. It offers practical steps to help you consistently execute your plans. Read it and WIN! $9.95

*Passionate Performance: Engaging Minds and Hearts to Conquer the Competition* by Lee J. Colan, offers practical strategies to engage the minds and hearts of your team at home, work, church or in the community. Read it and conquer your competition! $9.95

*Listen Up, Leader!* Ever wonder what employees think about their leaders? This book tells you the seven characteristics of leadership that people will follow. $9.95

*12 Choices ... That Lead to Your Success* is about success ... how to achieve it, keep it and enjoy it ... by making better choices. $14.95

*Management Insights* explores the myths and realities of management. It provides insight into how you can become a successful manager. $14.95

*Leadership ER* is a powerful story that shares valuable insights on how to achieve and maintain personal health, business health and the critical balance between the two. Read it and develop your own prescription for personal and professional health and vitality. $14.95

*CornerStone Leadership Collection of Quotations Calendar* is a compelling collection of quotes for leadership and life. Get a daily dose of inspiration with this perpetual calendar! $12.95

Visit www.**CornerStoneLeadership**.com
for additional books and resources.

# ✓ YES! Please send me extra copies of *Lessons in Loyalty!*

1-30 copies  $14.95      31-100 copies  $13.95      100+ copies  $12.95

Lessons in Loyalty _____ copies X _____ = $ _____

## Additional Leadership Development Resources

| | | |
|---|---|---|
| Monday Morning Leadership | ____ copies X $14.95 | = $ _____ |
| Monday Morning Leadership for Women | ____ copies X $14.95 | = $ _____ |
| Monday Morning Communications | ____ copies X $14.95 | = $ _____ |
| Sticking to It | ____ copies X $9.95 | = $ _____ |
| Passionate Performance | ____ copies X $9.95 | = $ _____ |
| Listen Up, Leader! | ____ copies X $9.95 | = $ _____ |
| 12 Choices ... That Lead to Your Success | ____ copies X $14.95 | = $ _____ |
| Management Insights | ____ copies X $14.95 | = $ _____ |
| Leadership ER | ____ copies X $14.95 | = $ _____ |
| CornerStone Quotations Calendar | ____ copies X $12.95 | = $ _____ |
| Loyalty Package | ____ packs X $139.95 | = $ _____ |
| (Includes all 11 items listed above.) | Shipping & Handling | $ _____ |
| | Subtotal | $ _____ |
| | Sales Tax (8.25%-TX Only) | $ _____ |
| | **Total (U.S. Dollars Only)** | $ _____ |

### Shipping and Handling Charges

| Total $ Amount | Up to $49 | $50-$99 | $100-$249 | $250-$1199 | $1200-$2999 | $3000+ |
|---|---|---|---|---|---|---|
| Charge | $6 | $9 | $16 | $30 | $80 | $125 |

Name _____ Job Title _____

Organization _____ Phone _____

Shipping Address _____ Fax _____

Billing Address _____ E-mail _____

City _____ State _____ Zip _____

❑ Please invoice (Orders over $200) Purchase Order Number (if applicable) _____

Charge Your Order:  ❑ MasterCard        ❑ Visa        ❑ American Express

Credit Card Number _____ Exp. Date _____

Signature _____

❑ Check Enclosed (Payable to: CornerStone Leadership)

| **Fax** | **Mail** | **Phone** |
|---|---|---|
| **972.274.2884** | **P.O. Box 764087** | **888.789.5323** |
| | **Dallas, TX 75376** | |

www.**CornerStoneLeadership**.com

CornerStone
Leadership Institute